GREENBERG'S
GUIDE TO
LIONEL TRAINS
1970 - 1997
Volume III: Accessories

GREENBERG'S
GUIDE TO
LIONEL TRAINS
1970 - 1997
Volume III: Accessories

Roland E. LaVoie

KALMBACH BOOKS

Printed in the United States of America

97 98 99 00 01 02 03 04 05 06   10 9 8 7 6 5 4 3 2 1

For more information, visit our website at
http://www.kalmbach.com

Publisher's cataloging in publication
(Prepared by Quality Books Inc.)

LaVoie, Roland, 1943–
        Greenberg's guide to Lionel trains, 1970–1997. Vol. III,
Accessories / Roland LaVoie.
        p. cm.
        Includes index.

        1. Railroads—Models. 2. Lionel Corporation. I. Greenberg
Publishing Company. II. Title. III. Title: Guide to Lionel
trains, 1979–1997. IV: Lionel trains, 1970–1997. V. Title:
Accessories.

        TF197.L38 1997   625.1'9
                                                        QBI95-20795

Book design: Sabine Beaupré
Cover design: Kristi Ludwig

CONTENTS

Dedication

With considerable good will and affection, I dedicate this book to Joe Gordon and Joe Bratspis, the proprietors of the Toy Train Station in Feasterville, Pennsylvania, as well as to all the members of the "Friday Night Irregulars," who have put up with my train collecting antics for the better part of the last fifteen years. Thanks, guys!

Acknowledgments

A book of this type could never come from the mind of one person (unless Thomas Jefferson had ever gotten the chance to play with Lionel trains!). All of these reference works are of a collaborative nature; this one is built on the foundation established by the chapter on accessories in the second volume of *Greenberg's Guide to Lionel Trains, 1970–1991*. Within that chapter, many individual collectors are cited, and their contributions continue. We welcome additional comments on any of the entries presented here; send a note to Kalmbach Publishing Co. if you want to correct an error, add some detail, or supply comments.

First of all, I want to thank Bruce and Linda Greenberg, who have been so encouraging to me on many levels for so long. This literate, intelligent couple has enriched my knowledge in many areas besides toy trains, and I count them among my best friends. Similarly, I could not have completed this book without the contributions of Tom Rollo, a perceptive collector of Lionel from Milwaukee and the best observer of details and patterns I have ever seen in the train hobby. Tom and I spent a few summer days in Sykesville, Maryland, with Bruce and Linda to sort out the basic organization of this book. Tom also was instrumental in formulating the cross-reference feature, which is entirely new in toy train publishing history. I am also indebted to Peter Riddle, a cultured Nova Scotia music professor, who has shared many ideas through his books about vintage toy trains and their wiring systems.

It doesn't stop there, either. Somehow, the staff of Greenberg Shows Inc. has managed to tolerate my oddball excesses during my participation in those shows. Space prohibits my listing individual names, but those people certainly know who they are. In another area, the proprietors and clientele of the Toy Train Station in Feasterville, Pennsylvania, have always been cooperative, even when I needed to search, mole-like, through store stock and packing boxes for that one item yet to be described here. These people include (but are not limited to) the proprietors, Joe Gordon and Joe Bratspis, and steady "Friday Night Irregulars," such as Joe Breitner, Fred Davis, Maury Friedrich, Denis Oravec, and many others who gladly share their considerable wisdom with me.

Perhaps most of all, there's my family: wife Jimmie, son Tom, and mom-in-law Louise, who must wonder about the sanity of someone who has six Hirsch shelves in the garage stacked floor to ceiling with toy trains, but who has to have that one more locomotive to add to them. Objectively, what does one say about middle-aged people who play with toy trains? In addition, there are my colleagues and students (past and present) at Cherry Hill High School East, some of whom are also toy train fans and others who, in their own ways, shake their heads and understand my magnificent obsession.

The production of a book doesn't stop with my writing the basic text, either. At Kalmbach Publishing Co., I had the assistance of several terrific people, including Roger Carp, the editor of this book, and Dick Christianson, who manages the Books Department. Photographer Bill Zuback spent two days with me shooting roll after roll of film in my stuffy garage for many of the photos used in this book. I didn't have the heart to tell him we forgot to take a picture of the Lionel boxer shorts I had in my upstairs den! In the production stage, many others helped prepare this book, notably Sabine Beaupré, who designed it; Kristi Ludwig, who designed the cover; Mary Algozin, copy editor; and Julie LaFountain, editorial assistant. I also appreciate being able to use catalog images through the courtesy of Lionel LLC.

When I was a college student, I had a dream of someday becoming a published author. However, in my wildest visions, I never foresaw that my books would be about Lionel trains! Being allowed to pursue the dreams treasured and collected in a person's heart is what makes life fulfilling. As I once more share a dream with you through a book I have written, I hope that your own life will be made just a little better. I know my own has been made very, very rich.

—Cherry Hill, New Jersey; November 1996

INTRODUCTION

A memorable song in the history of American popular music contains the line, "Everything old is new again." That little lyric is singularly appropriate for the task faced by the new purveyors of Lionel trains, General Mills, as the 1970 holiday season came around. Despite the promise of the Lionel name, General Mills faced some serious problems in its marketing efforts, mostly because the new firm found itself in competition with the old. How does a company market new crossing gates when there are thousands of older, unsold ones on the market? Even more important, how does a new venture with an established product create an identity for itself?

Those were not the new Lionel's only marketing problems. The market for toy trains had diminished drastically by the end of the 1960s, to the point where it was just barely alive when General Mills took over production. One major task of the new firm had to be the buildup for a whole new market for the trains. Accessories would have to wait for a while in terms of innovation. But what would Lionel do in the meantime for its consumers?

The answer concocted by General Mills was innovative and quite effective. The company directed its main efforts at the production of complete train sets to attract a new audience. Initially, that is where the innovative ideas, such as fast-angle wheel sets and the Electronic Sound of Steam, went. Lionel was able to do

this because it had inherited a huge warehouse of parts from the old Lionel Corporation. Beginning in 1971, that is where most of the accessories came from, including a few special items. In the first year, 1970, parts for accessories were thrown together where necessary just to keep the most common items available for purchase.

It made sense for the new Lionel to market its goods in this fashion. In the first place, the possession of a huge stockpile of ready-made accessory parts was "found money"; all the firm had to do was assemble the parts and sell them. In turn, that strategy bought considerable time for Lionel until some new accessories could be designed and tested. Through all of 1971 and 1972, the old parts (with a few restampings) kept Lionel's accessories alive and well in a slowly expanding toy train market. Meanwhile, the market itself was changing, and in 1973 the new Lionel discovered the vast potential collector's market, something Joshua Lionel Cowen had never exploited.

Once Lionel's stockpile of accessory parts was depleted, a decision had to be made concerning the new accessories to be marketed to spur collector and operator business. Here the associations of the new firm came in handy. General Mills owned a subsidiary hobby division known as Model Products Corporation (MPC). This division had become a skilled marketer of building kits, such as model airplanes. Therefore, the first accessory effort from the new firm became kits of railroad-related structures and buildings. There is no solid evidence to support the source of the designs for such 1973 kits as the Grain Elevator and the Rico Station, but many Lionel students believe that the designs for these buildings came from Pola, a European kit firm noted for its excellent designs in several scales.

Actually, there had been two previous efforts at marketing building structures, both of which were a lot more primitive than the Pola designs. In its early 1971 sets, Lionel included packaging materials molded in the shape of buildings. This was called Foam Village Packaging By Myco. Fully decorated pieces were modeled in the catalogs, but undecorated Styrofoam was all a consumer got. After this interesting but unsuccessful foray into free housing for train buffs, Lionel contracted with Bachmann Industries in Philadelphia to manufacture a few special assortments of kits based on its Plasticville line. The old Lionel Corporation had done this during the late 1950s, so it was not a new strategy. These building assortments were marketed only in 1971 and are difficult to find today. They are the Cross Country Set, Alamo Junction Set, and Whistle Stop Set. Frequently the buildings found in Lionel's kits were molded in the reverse colors of the regular Plasticville kits. Clearly, something better than these stopgap measures had to be added to the accessory line.

During 1973 and 1974, Fundimensions tried very hard to find a breakthrough accessory line that would expand sales. Unfortunately, its first two efforts did not bear fruit. In 1973 the firm introduced a revolutionary track system called Trutrack, designed to replace O and O27 gauge track. The pieces looked realistic, as they had many more plastic ties per section than did Lionel's traditional tubular track. Trutrack had flat surfaced rails and was fastened with clips, much like HO scale track. Manual and remote switches were to be available and, most significantly, realistic roadbed pieces were available to answer a pressing need that the old Lionel Corporation never addressed in the 1950s and '60s (despite the fact that rival American Flyer did). After manufacturing quite a bit of track and roadbed, Fundimensions pulled Trutrack from the market. Why? There has been much speculation. Initially, problems with the switches were blamed; later, collectors cited the system's incompatibility with Magnetraction (Trutrack had aluminum construction). The real reason most likely involved marketing rather than materials. Fundimensions probably found that the track and its components could not be manufactured economically enough to compete with its own and other track systems. Surviving pieces show that Trutrack would

have been an asset to Fundimensions and layout builders. The high manufacturing costs of components would return to plague the firm, finally causing the demise of the Fundimensions division in 1984 during a catastrophic move to Mexico.

Fundimensions also decided to get into non-powered preschool toy trains, with its Happy Huff 'N Puff and Gravel Gus sets. These sets, made of composition plastic and "powered by a child's imagination" (to quote the company's literature), were launched into the teeth of a strong market dominated by such giants of the industry as Fisher-Price and Playskool, which marketed similar toys. Fundimensions didn't stand much chance against that competition; gone were the days when Lionel could dictate the market. The preschool sets were soon withdrawn, and today they are hard-to-find curiosities of a company struggling to find its way into the toy marketplace. It would take another 20 years before a similar venture would be made by Lionel, this time successfully, in the form of Thomas The Tank Engine in large gauge and its many accessories.

In 1975 Fundimensions proved that it could successfully market an entirely new toy train accessory. The firm surprised everyone with the introduction of an operating drawbridge. Made to accommodate O27 track, the new drawbridge operated much like its illustrious predecessor, the 313 Bascule Bridge, although it did not resemble that massive icon of the postwar years. The drawbridge was difficult to wire and set up, but once in operation it worked well. Fundimensions even included the bridge in its Illinois Central Gulf set in 1976 and continued to offer it for several years thereafter.

During the late 1970s the toy train marketplace expanded to the point where serious collectors began to demand more complex and expensive sets of trains. In time, nostalgia for the great postwar accessories prompted Fundimensions to change its marketing strategy by offering Traditional and Collector lines in separate sections of its catalog. In 1980 the first stirrings of an accessory renaissance appeared with the production of O gauge switches just like their postwar predecessors and the 2301 Sawmill. Another sign of what was to come appeared in the form of the 2302 manually operated Gantry Crane. After that year, the floodgates burst. In the next three years, such venerated Lionel accessories as the oil derrick, newsstand, icing station, control tower and coaling station were produced, and all were received enthusiastically.

In late 1983 an issue of *USA Today*'s business section carried a startling headline: "Lionel Chugging to Mexico." General Mills, in tune with the business philosophy of the time, had decided to move its manufacturing facilities from Mount Clemens, Michigan, to a *maquiladora* facility just across the Mexican border. The move, designed to save labor costs, was a complete catastrophe for Fundimensions. Toy trains have always been complex, interdependent objects to manufacture because they are part of a complete system rather than one-of-a-kind toys. Severe delays in production soon occurred, in part because the language barrier was too much for the firm's supervisors to overcome. Lionel's customers began to complain about quality control, too; it wasn't unusual to find a piece of rolling stock or an accessory partially assembled within its sale box. Delays became a nightmare; the little and eagerly awaited Lionel trolley, for example, was scheduled to come out in 1984 but did not appear until two years later. The Mexican experiment was abandoned in 1985 and, after temporary warehousing in San Diego, the firm was back in Mount Clemens by the next year.

General Mills had by this time soured on the whole Lionel experience, and during 1986 the Lionel division was spun off briefly to the Kenner-Parker toy division. Enter Richard Kughn, a wealthy real estate entrepreneur from Detroit and lifelong Lionel devotee. He purchased the entire assets of Lionel and renamed the company Lionel Trains Incorporated (LTI). The second phase of the Modern Era was about to begin and with it some spectacular new accessory offerings.

Kughn's priority with Lionel was to take the line into some new and surprising directions. In his first catalog for 1987, LTI announced the motorized 12700 Erie gantry crane as well as a revival of the diesel fueling station and an entirely new line of Sidetracks peripherals. However, the best indicator of what was to come was the new, solid-state MW transformer. Although the design of the MW was not a great success, it directly led to a better RS-1 and eventually to an entirely new power system based on electronics, the TrainMaster Control System.

LTI also began to develop some amazing innovations. In 1988 it announced something truly revolutionary: RailScope. This incredible system featured a tiny television transmitter on the front of a handsome GP9 diesel locomotive. The camera inside the engine sent a black-and-white image back through the rails to a television set, where the image gave the viewer an "engineer's-eye" view of his own Lionel pike. Large and HO scale versions soon followed. Despite the great interest in the system, it had the fatal flaw of consuming 9-volt batteries at an alarming rate. LTI announced two RailScope locomotives in 1990 that used track power for the TV camera, but they were never produced, no doubt because their cost would

have been prohibitive. RailScope was a fascinating failure, but its production would soon bear fruit in several other areas.

During these years, besides offering old favorites, LTI expanded Lionel's accessory offerings into entirely new areas. In 1989 it produced the huge 12741 Intermodal Crane, which could travel on its own power, lift trailers off trucks and onto flat cars (and the reverse), and bring Lionel into modern railroad adventures. A new line of tractors and trailers was produced for use with the crane, but these little road vehicles assumed a popularity of their own. In 1990 a clever (if macabre) version of the old 445 Switch Tower was produced. The Burning Switch Tower featured scorch marks on its exterior, ominous blinking orange lights to simulate a fire, and a rather effective Seuthe smoke unit that gave a credible impression of a ghastly fire. This little accessory was so popular that LTI felt compelled to do a second run in 1993.

In the early 1990s new accessories appeared in profusion. A clever animated billboard that changed its signs emerged, along with a rather neat forklift loader station. Meanwhile, new animated freight and passenger stations were designed. Then largest accessory yet made emerged in 1991: the gigantic 12782 Operating Lift Bridge. It was made from an original design dating to 1950 that the old Lionel Corporation never produced. It even had its own separate power source! When activated, strobe lights flashed, bells rang, and warning horns blared as the bridge's center section was raised for "river traffic." The accessory came packed in a box so big it would not fit into many car trunks! It was a truly spectacular accessory on the largest of layouts.

LTI didn't stop there. A year later, it announced the 12767 Steam Clean and Wheel Grinding Shop. This accessory was revolutionary because it came in modular design and could be arranged in several ways on a layout. As locomotives passed through the steam cleaning facility, realistic smoke simulated the steam. A realistic wash rack (without the real water, of course!) was included, and lights simulated the sparks of the wheel grinding facility. Its flexibility of design made it extremely interesting to Lionel operators; clubs that featured modular sections at shows did much to popularize these complex accessories by demonstrating them.

During these years, Lionel faced stiff competition from many train manufacturing firms eager to bring tinplate railroading into a new world of electronic control. Such manufacturers as K-Line Electric Trains, QSI Industries, and Williams Reproductions designed new propulsion and sound systems. LTI proved itself capable of responding to these challenges, and the beneficiary has been the tinplate railroader, who now can choose components to satisfy every possible whim.

LTI was never afraid to experiment with new approaches to its accessories, even when they did not work out on a cost-efficiency basis. For example, the firm announced a train control/talking freight station that would have been a terrific animated accessory but could not be made economically enough for production. The same problem applied to a complex crossing gate and signal similar to units made in large scale by LGB. Significantly, LTI scrapped a planned revival of the venerable ZW transformer because it had something better and revolutionary in the works.

In late 1994 Lionel announced the second version of its electronic sound system, RailSounds II, which featured realistic steam and diesel sounds synthesized from real locomotives. This was sensational and possibly the best sound system ever produced for tinplate, but LTI's follow-up to it pulled the temple pillars down and broke with tradition. This was the TrainMaster Control System, an all-electronic power and control system that could run a nearly unlimited number of trains and accessories through a handheld walkaround controller. Its complex components include a Power House transformer unit, Power Master Command Center, TrainMaster Command Base, Wireless Remote Control, "Big Red Button" to repeat programmed commands, and Switch-Accessory Controller. Locomotives designed to use this system can do more tricks than a circus acrobat. Cars can be uncoupled, switches moved, and accessories triggered from one handheld control. Incredibly, the system is compatible with all older Lionel equipment, and operators can run several trains on one track safely and efficiently, with each train responding to different commands. The TrainMaster Control System is truly a state-of-the-art design that will keep Lionel competitive with anyone.

As Lionel's accessories approach the brave new world of electronic control and the firm reaches its centennial, we should reflect on what the modern era really means. Despite all the innovation, the essential purpose of Lionel's accessories has remained remarkably consistent. That purpose is the creation of a microcosm, or "little world," that can be animated and controlled as a railroader's personal little empire. In the 1950s one of Lionel's slogans was "Control of Lionel Trains today . . . Control of his life tomorrow." It illustrates the true function of these magnificent accessories. In a world where so much seems out of control, here is one little corner of it that is entirely

the creation and responsibility of the model railroader. From the first days of Lionel Trains, that has been the real appeal of the firm's efforts. Every once in a while, Lionel forgets that purpose, usually to its own grief. However, at its best Lionel has enabled thousands of model railroaders to realize their dreams of a miniature empire. Those dreams will keep Lionel's trains and accessories alive and well into their second hundred years. As we've said, "Everything old is new again."

This book has been divided into twelve chapters by categories. Each chapter contains an introduction and a listing of accessory items by number. Since much modern-era equipment is new or in better shape than postwar, values are given for pieces in Excellent and Mint conditions.

"Mint" means absolutely new and unused, with all original boxes, packing materials, wires, and so forth, as well as instruction sheets. A piece is *not* mint if it does not meet those stringent requirements. The item may have been taken out of its box and examined, but it should show no signs of wear whatsoever.

"Excellent" means free of scratches and cosmetic flaws despite some evidence of use. Many collectors think this category should include the original box; others do not.

"Like New" items are valued somewhere between Excellent and Mint. Items more worn but in "Very Good" condition would command about 60 to 75 percent of "Excellent" values.

The toy train marketplace, like any other one, is driven by supply and demand. If you are relatively new to the world of Lionel, it is in your interest to shop around and be patient before purchasing an accessory. If you have any reservations about a particular piece, we *strongly* urge that you consult a reliable and experienced collector before purchase. Most collectors, realizing that the availability of accessories relies upon value for the money, will be glad to assist you.

Within chapters, items are listed numerically, along with a description of appearance and operating tips and maintenance suggestions where applicable. References are given for an accessory's postwar and modern-era predecessors and successors. For example, the 2133 Freight Station has PW (postwar) 132 and 133 ancestors and ME (modern-era) 12728 and 12782 successors. If you cannot find one version of a given accessory, these cross references may help you find a similar accessory for your needs. Good luck and happy Lionel railroading!

1

STATIONS AND SIGNAL TOWERS

A very common circumstance in the late nineteenth century was that individuals who wanted train service to places near their homes would actually finance the building of a station themselves if the railroad would agree to stop trains there. . . . Private construction of suburban stations resulted in some of the most comely and pleasing stations built in the nineteenth century.
—George H. Douglas, *All Aboard!*
The Railroad in American Life

INTRODUCTION

Wayside stations have been part of Lionel's heritage since the very beginning of the firm in early 1901. Perhaps this is because these stations represent the romance of the railroad so well. After all, for most of Lionel's history the small-town depot was a place where young boys could follow their dreams. The arrival of either the *Overland Limited* or a humble peddler freight was a big event in those simpler times. Arrivals and departures would be duly noted; the unique sounds and voices of a train making a stop are familiar still within many people's memories. One would dream of the train's destination in the magical Big City with all its allurements before the familiar simplicity of small-town life would reassert itself.

Joshua Lionel Cowen knew a lot about the alluring nature of those dreams. Even in the very early catalogs, you could find magnificent tinplate stations sold under Lionel's name but undoubtedly of German origin. Then there followed the beautifully enameled depots of the prewar years, such as the beautifully lighted 124 Station and 115 Depot with Train Control. In the postwar years the stations became animated with little

baggage carts scurrying in and out of the baggage rooms. They still had magic, even if plastic had long since replaced enameled metal.

Perhaps unintentionally, Fundimensions paid homage to that station heritage with one of its first models, the 2156 Station Platform of 1971. In keeping with its efficient policy of using up inherited parts, the firm equipped this one-year-only station with some old lamps from the late prewar era. When it exhausted the supply of lamps, Fundimensions replaced this rather pretty platform with the nonilluminated 2256. A fine revival of the postwar 133 followed in several interesting variations.

These models have since appeared in many permutations, but perhaps the most interesting variant is one that was never produced—the proposed 12762 Freight Station With Control And Sounds. Essentially, this was to have been a modernized version of the old American Flyer Talking Station, a very successful accessory for The A. C. Gilbert Co. in the 1940s and 1950s. It was to include a train-stopping thermostat control, like the one in the postwar Lionel 132 and some sort of voice mechanism for train announcements. Presumably the station could not be made economically enough, so it was never produced. Maybe in the future a version will be considered that incorporates a microcassette recorder so the owner of the accessory can make up his or her own announcements. *That* would be a truly interesting accessory!

Fundimensions and Lionel Trains Inc. also paid considerable attention to signal and switch towers. Fundimensions produced both nonoperating and operating versions of the postwar 445 with its two active little crewmen, and LTI came up with a clever, if gruesome, variation of this tower, the Burning Switch

Tower, which incorporated a smoke unit to simulate a fire. The postwar 192 Control Tower, with its dispatchers inexplicably running around in circles, has been revived in several variations, as has the rotating radar tower in case the modern operator has any low-flying planes. LTI also marketed new and amusingly animated freight and passenger stations based upon the operating mechanism of the Animated Refreshment Stand.

By any estimate, modern-era Lionel has paid attention to the allure of the trackside station. As long as railroads are modeled, no operating pike would be complete without them. They stand as clear testimony to the rich heritage of tinplate railroading's past.

2129 FREIGHT STATION, 1983–85

Brick red platform, tan building with brown windows and door, green roof, black picket fence with billboards reading Cheerios, Wheaties, and Gold Medal. Also several wall posters, illuminated by one interior bulb. The catalog shows the station with white walls. 15" long, 5" wide, and 5½" high. The 2129 was the modern era's first attempt to bring back one of the best sellers of the postwar era. It was soon followed by an operating version, the 2323, and it featured new and brighter colors. The fence was redesigned to accept

stick-on advertising posters instead of the old metal folding signs. The old 57 lamp was retained for illumination. **Cross-references:** PW 256, 356; ME 2323.

35   40

2133 FREIGHT STATION, 1972–83

Maroon plastic base, white plastic sides; box at one time made by Stone Container Corp., Detroit, white corrugated box with picture of station on lid (except (A) below). Earliest versions use metal clip-on bayonet-base light socket, rather than the postwar version, in which the light socket is riveted to the bracket. Later Fundimensions stations have plastic clip-on socket using a 12-volt automotive-type bulb. T. Rollo comment. This station is a fine revival of the late-model 133 of the postwar years. It shows clearly the progression of manufacturing techniques of the modern era and is available in several interesting variations, a few of which are difficult to find. The basic colors, as with the postwar version, are maroon, white, and green, but the green is noteworthy for variations. The chimney on the roof is always green, unlike the postwar versions, which usually have red-brick chimneys. Close attention should be paid to the Stone Container Corp. box and the type of lightbulb fastening, two features that help identify variations. The presence or absence of a

The 2133 Freight Station revived the illuminated stop stations that had been vital parts of the Lionel line through much of the postwar era. The earliest version (A), which dates from the first part of 1972, came in a white box with a drawing on it; the box was made by the Stone Container Corp.

Exc   Mint

quarter-sized hole in the base also distinguishes early from late models. Some samples have cream-colored walls instead of white, but this is most likely a function of aging rather than a specific variation. **Cross-references:** PW 132, 133; ME 12728, 12762, 12812.

(A) First production, 1972: white Stone Container Corp. box with no picture on lid (though space is there for it). Example has bright metal cross-piece for bulb clip, small red and gold station end signs, and bright green roof. Quarter-sized hole in floor, last seen in 1966 version of 133, is retained. R. LaVoie Collection.

35   45

(B) Later production, 1972; Stone Container box with black-and-white picture of accessory, medium green roof [not as bright as (A)], door, and window inserts, quarter-sized hole in base, green chimney secured by circular speed nut, black metal interior crossbar, bayonet-base metal light socket clips to bar. R. LaVoie Collection.

35   45

(C) Same as (B), but red chimney instead of green. Probable use of leftover postwar part. G. Halverson Collection.

35   45

Exc   Mint

(D) Later production, 1973–75; Stone Container box has color picture of accessory, pea green roof, chimney, doors, and window inserts, maroon base, previous hole in base is filled, chimney secured by rectangular speed nut, black metal interior crossbar, plastic light socket taking automotive-type bulb clips onto crossbar. T. Rollo and G. Halverson Collections.

25   35

(E) Latest production 1976–83, same as (D), but dull Penn Central green roof, chimney, doors, and window inserts, red-brown base, gray metal crossbar inside station. R. LaVoie Collection.

25   35

2156 STATION PLATFORM, 1971

Pea green plastic base modeled after 156, medium red roof, illuminated by two large prewar acorn lightbulbs, underside of base reads, "CAT. NO. 2156 STATION PLATFORM" and "LIONEL MT. CLEMENS MICH. MADE IN USA." Mint value must have original lightbulbs and Type I box. Hard to find with original lightbulbs. This station platform features an extremely interesting amalgamation of prewar, postwar and

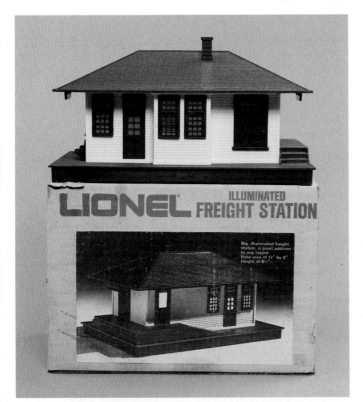

Left: Starting in the latter part of 1972, the 2133 Freight Station (B) came in a white box on which a black-and-white photo of the accessory was pasted; the box was still made by the Stone Container Corp. Right: The photo on the box changed to color, beginning with version D in 1973. The color of the roof also was modified to a lighter shade of green (pea green from 1973 to 1975 and Penn Central green from 1976 to 1983).

Every passenger terminal needs plenty of station platforms, so Lionel has regularly cataloged this accessory. Left: The postwar 156 returned in 1971 as the 2156, which featured lightbulbs left over from the late prewar period. Right: In 1973 the 2156 was replaced by the 2256, which lacked illumination. The last version (D) was packaged in an unusual box from the Stone Container Corp.

	Exc	Mint

modern-era components, perhaps the only such combination of its kind. Electrically, it is set up like the prewar and postwar 156 platform, but its metal posts are newly made; its lightbulbs date from the late 1930s; and its roof and platform are injection-molded plastic rather than the painted compression-molded plastic of the 156. Like several of its early modern-era contemporaries, it is now difficult to find, since it was cataloged for only one year. **Cross-references:** PW 156, 157; ME 2256, 2292, 12731, 12748. R. LaVoie and T. Rollo Collections.

	45	60

2256 STATION PLATFORM, 1973–81

Green plastic base, metal posts, black plastic center fence, red unpainted plastic roof, not illuminated. Although the metal supports remain in this 2156-like station platform, their sockets are blind and not machined for lightbulbs, and this version is nonilluminated. Typically the red and green colors are much brighter than those of their predecessor. The Type I box of the 2156 is replaced by a windowless Type II box, and sometimes a minor variation of the 2256 can be found that uses a leftover 2156 base. **Cross-references:** PW 156, 157; ME 2156, 2292, 12731, 12748

	Exc	Mint
(A) As described above.	20	25

(B) Train Collectors Association special issue: Penn Central green base, lighter red roof than regular issue, overprint heat-stamped in white; 21st T. C. A. National Convention, Orlando, Florida, June 26–29, 1975. G. Halverson and R. LaVoie Collections.

	25	35

(C) Same as (A), but leftover 2156 light green base. Fairly common variation. R. LaVoie Collection.

	20	25

(D) Same as (A), but came in unusual Stone Container Corp. corrugated box with red and black wraparound label on one side and both ends. R. LaVoie Collection.

	25	35

2292 STATION PLATFORM, 1985–87

Dark red base, black plastic roof supports, black fencing, dark green roof, chromed acorn nut roof fasteners; nonilluminated. This station platform came knocked down in a small box for assembly by the consumer rather than ready-made. It is somewhat smaller than its predecessors. **Cross-references:** PW 156, 157; ME 2156, 2256, 12731, 12748.

	6	10

Left: One version (C) of the 2256 Station Platform included the light green base that originally was used on the 2156. Right: In 1975 the Train Collectors Association offered a special version (B) of the 2256 to commemorate its national convention, held in Orlando, Florida.

Exc   Mint

2318 CONTROL TOWER, 1983–84

Yellow building, black superstructure, gray base (postwar 192 predecessor had orange and green colors). Two men move in circles around the building interior; powered by vibrator motor. Reissued in new colors with new number in 1987 and 1995. This revival of the 192 is interesting for several reasons. There were actually two different runs of the accessory: the first, with a red roof, was produced in Mexico; the second, with a maroon roof, was made in Mount Clemens. Neither version had a protective aluminum strip above the lightbulb, so these two runs of the accessory were subject to melted roofs unless they were modified. The socket cannot be bent down because the figures pass under it. To prevent roof damage, replace the 14-volt lightbulb supplied with the accessory with an 18-volt bayonet bulb. Fasten aluminum foil, shiny side out, to the underside of the roof just above the lightbulb. Later versions produced by LTI had an aluminum protective shield. **Cross-references:** PW 192; ME 12702, 12878.

(A) Red tower roof, Mexican production. Possibly scarcer than (B), but more reader observations needed. R. LaVoie Collection.

65   80

(B) Maroon tower roof, Mount Clemens production.

65   80

The 2292, an attractive model of the station platform with a dark red base and no illumination, came in pieces as part of an easily assembled structure.

2319 WATCH TOWER, 1975–80

White body, maroon base and staircase, Penn Central green roof, red chimney, green door and window inserts. This nonoperating version of the postwar

A favorite from the postwar era, the operating freight station made its return to the Lionel line in 1984 with the 2323. It featured new colors and advertisements. Considering that General Mills owned Lionel, the ads for Cheerios, Wheaties, and Gold Medal flour made perfect sense.

	Exc	Mint

445 looks threadbare without its operating components because the parts still retain all the operating slots. The plastic used for this version is noticeably translucent. The watch tower came in a windowless Type II box and was illuminated by a 12-volt automotive-type bulb in a clip-on plastic socket. **Cross-references:** PW 445; ME 2324, 12768, 12917.

25 35

2323 OPERATING FREIGHT STATION, 1984–85

Dark red base, black metal baggage cart pathway, light tan housing, dark green roof, two green luggage carts, stick-on billboards, black fence with poster ads (postwar 356 had metal signs, while this model has modified fence to accommodate stick-on posters). This was the operating version of the 356, done up in the same colors as the nonoperating 2129 released the year before. Baggage carts move around the station in alternation (Both carts are dark green and have reinforcement pieces added to a top rod that retains the cart inside the station, where it is released by a trip

device). Earliest production suffered from warped bases. These will operate properly with careful adjustment of the base retaining screws. The carts do not seem to work as well as their postwar predecessors. **Cross-references:** PW 256, 356; ME 2129.

75 100

2324 OPERATING SWITCH TOWER, 1984–85

Dark red base, steps, and upper doorway, tan building with dark brown door and window inserts, brown balcony, dark green roof with red chimney. The color scheme of the 2129 and 2323 Stations was used for this revival of the postwar 445. Operation was improved by the addition of a little metal ferrule for the line controlling the man who runs down the stairs; previous versions often jammed where the line passes through the tower wall. The figures have a tendency to come loose from their bracket slots. One man runs into the station house; the other comes downstairs; illuminated. Postwar man on stairs carries lantern in left hand; this version has a right-handed man. Some examples observed with left-handed man; probable use of leftover figures, even this long after postwar years. Somewhat neglected because of issue of "burning" variety, but this version is scarcer than generally thought. **Cross-references:** PW 445; ME 2319, 12768, 12917.

                                                    65   85

12702 OPERATING CONTROL TOWER, 1987

Red tower house with black roof and platform, black base, red ladders, gray superstructure with red LIONEL. White arrow and weathervane atop roof. LTI improved the familiar operating control tower in two ways: attractive new colors and a reflective underside to the roof to prevent burn-through, which had plagued earlier models produced in postwar and Fun-

dimensions versions. It's still a good idea to replace the 14-volt bayonet bulb supplied with the accessory with an 18-volt one. **Cross-references:** PW 192; ME 2318, 12878.

                                                    75   90

12728 ILLUMINATED FREIGHT STATION, 1989

Yellow-brown building with dark brown base and light brown roof, windows and doors, illuminated. This version of the late 2133 model is identical in construction but with different colors; the new colors follow the same pattern of changes found in the 2323 and 2324 accessories. **Cross-references:** PW 132, 133; ME 2133, 12762, 12812.

                                                    30   40

During the modern era, different revivals of the postwar operating switch tower have been offered. Left: A nonoperating version appeared first, the 2319, cataloged from 1975 to 1980. Center: Four years later, the 2324, an operating version, was introduced. Right: Lionel Trains doctored up this accessory in an unusual manner in 1990 to transform it into the 12768 Burning Switch Tower, complete with smoke and scorch marks.

Left: The 12749 Rotary Radar Antenna, cataloged by Lionel Trains Inc. from 1989 to 1991, was one among many postwar accessories revived in slightly different colors. Right: Another item descended from a postwar model was the 2318 Control Tower. The initial version (A) was manufactured in Mexico and featured a red roof.

	Exc	Mint

12731 STATION PLATFORM, 1988–95

Red roof, dark green base, black roof supports, signs on fence include Coca-Cola and Lionel, three chromed acorn nuts fasten supports to roof. Similar to Fundimensions 2292, except for color differences and different signboards on the fence. Packaged in knock-down form in Type VI box; minor assembly required. **Cross-references:** PW 156, 157; ME 2156, 2256, 2292, 12748.

10   15

	Exc	Mint

12748 ILLUMINATED STATION PLATFORM, 1989–95

Light gray base, black plastic roof supports and fence, dark red roof, press-on posters supplied for fence. This version of the small station platform is noteworthy for an ingenious lighting system. Two hoods, apparently from the mold used for the goose-neck street lamps, are mounted to the underside of the roof, and frosted L19-type pin-based bulbs are used for illumination. Their lighting is effective, and groups of these little platforms in a line can make up a great-looking train platform for a large layout. **Cross-references:** PW 156, 157; ME 2156, 2256, 2292, 12731.

20   25

12749 ROTARY RADAR ANTENNA, 1989–92, 1995

Gray tower structure, maroon tower base and top, gray radar antenna and radio pole; vibrator motor makes antenna rotate. This revival of a good postwar accessory is done in handsome colors, but does have a few operating problems. The rotating radar head sits in its socket at an angle, which means the back of the base of the antenna rubs against the socket base. To relieve that friction, apply dry Teflon-based lubricant to the friction points. This reduces the friction and allows the antenna to rotate freely. The accessory tends to be a bit noisy in operation. **Cross-reference:** PW 197.

40   50

12762   FREIGHT STATION WITH TRAIN CONTROL AND SOUNDS, 1990–91

Catalog shows white building modeled after 2133, light gray roof, doors, and windows, black base, interior light, smoke and thermostat train-stop device. This intriguing accessory was cataloged in 1990 and 1991, Book One, but it was never made. According to the catalog, the station was to revive the postwar thermostatic train-stopping device used in the 132 Station and 253 Block Signal. Three separate recordings were to announce arrivals and departures. It is not certain what kind of sound system was to be used; whatever it was, the accessory probably could not be mass-produced economically. If such an accessory is ever produced, it will be interesting to observe the sound system employed. American Flyer and Noma produced talking stations in the 1950s that relied on a small plastic record played by a makeshift phonograph device; this would be too primitive for today's sophisticated electronics. Perhaps a microcassette recorder system could be used. **Cross-references:** PW 132, 133; ME 2133, 12728, 12812

Not manufactured

12768 BURNING SWITCH TOWER, 1990 and 1993

Light tan building with dark brown window, door and deck trim, darker brown roof and black "scorch marks" weathered into plastic. Four connections under base lead to two switches, one for the action of the figures and one for the smoke unit. First and second productions identical except for lightbulbs used. This in-

ventive accessory was modeled after the 445 and 2324 models, but there the resemblance stops. The action of this accessory is clever and has made it a hot (excuse the pun!) seller. When one button is pressed, a second orange lamp is lit in the bottom level of the tower (another in the top is constantly lit). A smoke generator is activated, which pours copious quantities of smoke out the top story as a thermostat allows the second orange light to blink and flicker, simulating a fire. A second button sends two hand-painted figures into action: Hector (Lionel's name!) runs—rather foolishly—into the blazing building while Charles scurries down the side steps, carrying a water bucket to fight the flames. Many operators combine this tower with a motorized fire-fighting car on a nearby track for sustained action. Lionel's new smoke formulation works well in this accessory, as does LGB's smoke fluid because the smoke generator is a Seuthe-type common in many large-scale products. This is a somewhat melodramatic but very clever and popular accessory. In fact, such was its popularity that Lionel felt compelled to reissue it three years after it had first appeared. The second version featured a revised lighting system that used grain-of-wheat bulbs in plastic sockets rather than the first version's no. 53 bayonet-base bulbs. In both cases the bulbs are painted a heat-resistant orange. Both versions work well, but the second one's bulbs tend to burn out more easily at higher voltage. It is also easy to flood the smoke unit; excess smoke fluid should be drained and then no more than seven drops placed in the unit. With this treatment, the smoke produced is absolutely volcanic! **Cross-references:** PW 445; ME 2319, 2324, 12917.

(A) First production, 1990.

100   125

(B) Reissue, 1993.

85   100

12791 ANIMATED PASSENGER STATION, 1991

Red-brown base, raised light tan platform with black supports and light green open roof, cubic red cover to conceal motor, light tan freight truck, gray attendant with pieces of baggage on dolly, male and female passenger figures, black fencing and 2170 Lamp Post next to open shed. Although this whimsical accessory uses the same mechanism as the 12719 Refreshment Stand of 1989, its action is more surreal, especially at high voltage. When a button is pressed, a man in a blue suit moves back and forth, anxiously checking his timetable, a woman in a brown overcoat revolves frantically and looks both ways for the train, and an attendant spins a baggage cart around as if he can't quite decide what to do with it. Although the

The Animated Passenger Station injects more action into an O or O27 gauge layout. LTI cataloged this
amusing accessory for only a single year, perhaps because of flaws in its design.

Exc   Mint

action of the accessory is charming, the green 2170 Lamp Post seems attached to the station as an afterthought, the roof supports seem fragile and the whole accessory appears as if were something a very junior employee dreamed up to play with—which is, perhaps, the point! **Cross-reference:** ME 12818.

75   90

12812 FREIGHT STATION WITH LIGHTS, 1993–97

Structure and lighting identical to 12728. Brown base, door and window inserts, light tan walls, green roof with brown chimney. Despite a slight name change, this station is virtually identical to its predecessors except for its colors. Unlike other varieties, it must be partially assembled, which is a simple matter,

since door and window inserts are snapped into place quickly. **Cross-references:** PW 132, 133; ME 2133, 12728, 12762.

30   35

12818 ANIMATED FREIGHT STATION, 1992 and 1994

Brown base, light tan baggage platform, brown crate covers motor mechanism, black fencing and roof supports, green roof, small foil "LIONELVILLE" signs on roof supports, attached green 2170 Lamp Post, which lights only when accessory is activated (Memories of the 2125 Whistle Shack!). This is a freight variation of the previously produced 12791 Animated Passenger Station, with the same general

A year after introducing the 12791 Animated Passenger Station in 1991, LTI brought out the 12818 Animated Freight Station. This accessory also featured plenty of movement and charm, with figures turning and twisting endlessly. Operators liked both of these animated items and used them to liven up their model railroads.

Exc   Mint

structure and attached 2170 Lamp Post. In this case the somewhat wacky action involves a man pulling a cart up and down an inclined ramp, a man with a barrel-loaded dolly waiting his turn up the ramp by weaving back and forth, and a third figure with a crate on his shoulder revolving restlessly. In operation the baggage cart can detach itself from its hauler-person easily unless it is carefully secured. **Cross-reference:** ME 12791.

75   90

walls, clear windows and two revolving blue-clad dispatcher figures. This control tower appears to be identical to the 12702, except for different colors. As with the other versions, the figures running around their plot boards in frantic circles create quite a bit of whimsy and, at times, offer sardonic commentary about the efficiency (or lack thereof) in modern railroad control centers. **Cross-references:** PW 192; ME 2318, 12702.

60   80

12878 ILLUMINATED CONTROL TOWER, 1995

Gray base, platform and roof, black tower structure with yellow "LIONEL" lettering, red ladders and

12917 OPERATING SWITCH TOWER, 1996–97

Red-brown base, dark gray structure walls, dark brown roof, upper balcony, stairs and door and window

During the modern era, postwar accessories have been reissued more than once, with only their color schemes changed. That was the case with the 12878 Illuminated Control Tower, an updated version of the 12702. LTI made the 12878 available in 1995 with darker colors than its predecessor.

inserts, two blue figures with painted hands and faces, upper-level illumination. The catalog photo shows a nonburning(!) operating tower identical to the 2324 except for color. However, the illustration shows the man on the stairs carrying the lantern in his left hand (like

the man in the postwar 445 but unlike the figure in the 2324, who carried the lantern in his right hand). Another change involves the addition of a door on the upper platform; now the figure comes out the door rather than just flying through an opening. The most important change, however, is the operating mechanism. Instead of a solenoid, Lionel LLC uses a gear box powered by a small can motor. This provides for smoother operation and ends once and for all the annoying maintenance problem of restringing the cord through the projection rod inside the tower. The production model may differ from the one shown in the catalog. **Cross-references:** PW 445; ME 2319, 2324, 12768.

CP

12921 LIONEL RAILROADER CLUB ILLUMINATED STATION PLATFORM, 1995

Same as regular-production issue with lights: maroon roof, black supports, gray platform. This special issue lighted station is identical to the regular-production issue except for the inscription "LRRC 1995" in white on both ends of the roof and a set of special stickers for the advertising boards. Its only box was the actual shipping carton. **Cross-references:** ME 12748, 12812.

30   40

12960 ROTARY RADAR ANTENNA, 1997

Same colors as postwar predecessor: gray base, black tower structure, orange tower top, gray rotating unit. This reissue of the 197 is portrayed in the catalog as closely resembling its postwar equivalent in color. The operational cautions and tips from 12749 apply to this reissue as well. **Cross-references:** PW 197; ME 12749.

CP

52100 LCCA UNLIGHTED STATION PLATFORM, 1996

Maroon roof, black supports, gray base, special stickers for advertising boards. Essentially the same description as 12921 above, except unlighted, unassembled, and packed in Lionel Classic Type V box. **Cross-references:** ME 12731, 12748, 12812

CP

2

CARGO TRANSFER ACCESSORIES

In the link and pin days, freight cars had only hand brakes and link and pin couplers; this meant that cars had to be coupled by hand. One yardmaster asked a gang of transient brakemen and switchmen looking for work to hold out their hands. If the applicants had several fingers missing, the yardmaster knew they were "old-timers" and would be able to do the job. . . .
— B. A. Botkin and Alvin F. Harlow, Eds.,
A Treasury of Railroad Folklore

INTRODUCTION

In the 1936 movie *Things to Come,* art director William Cameron Menzies fully realized H. G. Wells's vision of the future by creating cities where power reigned supreme. Huge dynamos whirred endlessly, and eccentric gears two stories high thrashed with energy. Sparks and dust flew everywhere, and helmeted men piloted huge torpedo-shaped mining machines to wrest minerals out of the earth in a shower of electric arcs and sparks. Transport vehicles, autogyros, and private flying automobiles traveled in three dimensions, docking at the most futuristic of spaceports. Menzies created a vision of muscle, power, and brute brawn. It was the absolute pinnacle of the Age of the Machine.

That is a world Joshua Lionel Cowen understood perfectly. He could no more imagine his miniature train world without the honest work of heavy industry than we could imagine today's world without the microprocessor and the Internet. Although railroads certainly moved people, their prime function was to move cargo in huge quantities for a busy nation. That involved railroads interacting with other transportation modes, factories, warehouses, and all kinds of industrial facilities. Of all the accessories Lionel offered throughout its long history, the cargo transfer accessories are the ones that set it apart from other toy train

manufacturers; no one even came close to Lionel's offerings. The importance of this is that accessories which transferred cargo enabled young people to imitate the Machine Age they saw around them.

One of the most awe-inspiring aspects of heavy industry has always been the sheer size of its operations. The steam locomotives of a bygone era were hissing behemoths, and their successor diesels growled just as hugely in a child's imagination. With the simple push of a button, a child could move tons of coal, lift mammoth steel ingots with a magnetic crane, send barrels and logs to multiple destinations and tap oil fields — in the imagination, a direct imitation of the Machine Age world.

It was Lionel's clever engineering that made this fantasy world possible. In the postwar era, many cargo transfer accessories were powered by big, rugged, and reliable AC motors that growled noisily, just as real-sized motors did. In addition, the clever vibrator motor mechanism made objects move realistically with a strong-sounding buzz. Real machines made noise; so did Lionel's. There were coaling stations, lumber mills, oil derricks, gantry cranes, icing stations — all the devices toy train operators needed to create their own versions of the Machine Age.

It took a while for Fundimensions to reissue some of these great accessories, but when they finally did so, they created worthy successors to the lumber mill, oil derrick, icing and coaling stations, and gantry cranes. When Lionel Trains Inc. took over the line in 1987, it didn't just carry on this trend; it also created new, more modern accessories to mimic the changed world of industrial technology. One of the most striking of this new generation was the massive Intermodal Crane, designed to work with TOFC (Trailer On Flat Car) loads. This incredible device could straddle two tracks, move up and down the sidings under its own power, turn left

Fundimensions wisely revived a couple of the best American Flyer accessories. S and O gauge operators alike enjoy the 2300 Oil Drum Loader, which was cataloged from 1983 to 1987.

or right, and load and unload whole trailers from flatcars or trailer frames. It was spectacular in operation, even if it was awfully big for the average home layout. Another clever new cargo transfer accessory was the Fork Lift Loader Station, which cleverly created the illusion of a forklift truck hustling into and out of a shed while loading a double-door boxcar with lengths of pipe.

LTI also introduced a sealed can motor as a power source for many of these accessories. It may not have the comforting roar or buzz of the AC motor, the solenoid, or the vibrator, but this small motor is quite rugged and dependable as a power source. It needs far less attention from its user, too — a major advantage, since the AC motors need periodic oiling and lubrication and the vibrator motors tend to slip out of adjustment too easily.

Perhaps, in the real world, the time for the Machine Age has passed. However, even in the brave new world of the Information Age, there is still a true fascination with the power of making cargo move, either for real or in miniature. The psychological feeling of empowerment given to young children by these wonderful miniature machines assures that Lionel will continue to nurture and produce them.

2300 OIL DRUM LOADER, 1983–87

Red-brown base and ramp structure, yellow shed walls (without the black striping on the American Flyer original), green roof, red lift truck with painted human figure, six metal oil drums. This is a well-designed and entertaining revival of the successful Flyer

Exc   Mint

trackside accessory no. 779, cataloged in 1955 and 1956. When the button is pressed, a forklift truck scurries to a ramp alongside the structure concealing the operating motor. It tilts a metal barrel onto its loading platform and scoots across the deck, ultimately tipping the barrel into a waiting gondola on the train. At least, that's the theory! In practice, the loader is a real challenge to operate because the new can motor powering it is sensitive to voltage. If the lift truck scoots away from the ramp too quickly, the barrel will fall off the truck. With practice, the operator can vary the voltage to just the right level; each example seems to be different. This accessory is a great deal of fun for children—and it will certainly help them develop their fine motor skills, in more ways than one! **Cross-references:** Flyer 779; ME 12862.

100   150

2301 OPERATING SAW MILL, 1980–84

Dark gray plastic base, white mill building, red door, gray shed, red lettering on window facing track, white crane; 10½" long, 6" wide, 6" high. This interesting accessory creates the illusion of sawing logs into dressed lumber. When logs are dumped into a built-in tray (preferably by a trackside log dump car to add to the illusion), they are taken into the building by conveyor belt to the accompaniment of a loud buzz from the vibrator motor, which sounds like a saw. Meanwhile, on the other side of the building, five pine planks emerge, as if the logs had just been sawed. What really happens is that the logs drop into a rear compartment

while the planks have been previously loaded through a slot in the roof. The action is accomplished by a long reel of 35mm film with prongs attached to catch the logs and planks. Keep the operating voltage down; otherwise the logs, planks, or both can jam and stop up the accessory. The device is a clever illusion that works well for the most part. **Cross-references:** PW 464; ME 12873.

100   150

2302 UNION PACIFIC MANUAL GANTRY CRANE, 1981–82

Maroon crane housing and boom, Union Pacific markings, black platform spans track and runs on its own wheels. This was the first reissue of the fabled crane of the postwar years, but it was not mechanized. Operators worked it much as they would the manually operated crane cars; by rotating a rear and side wheel, they could raise and lower the hook and tilt the boom. The cab rotated too, but only by hand. Still, this and the next entry gave Lionel fans hope that a motorized version would soon appear. They were not to be disappointed. **Cross-reference:** ME 2303.

20   25

2303 SANTA FE MANUAL GANTRY CRANE, 1980–81

Dark blue plastic cab, yellow boom and Santa Fe lettering, gray superstructure. See comments for 2302. This version was not offered for separate sale; it came

The 2301 Operating Saw Mill is, except for its number, all but identical to its postwar predecessor.

Exc   Mint

as a kit in the no. 1072 Cross Country Express set. **Cross-reference:** ME 2302.

25   35

2305 OIL DERRICK, 1981–83

Walking beam rocks up and down, bubbling pipe simulates oil flow, hand-operated winch and hook; ladder, barrels, red-painted sheet metal base; Getty signs instead of Sunoco; slightly darker green tower structure; Type V box lacks gloss coating of most such boxes. Somewhat difficult to find in last few years. This was one of the first significant Fundimensions revivals of favorite postwar accessories; it was a duplicate of the original except for its new decorative scheme. A thermostatic device controls the speed of the grasshopper pump, and a 14-volt lamp heats a viscous liquid in a sealed tube that bubbles like an oil flow. Operationally the device can be finicky; the thermostat must be adjusted (an easy operation) for best rocking motion of the pump. In addition, the glass tube, quite fragile, must be just touching the lamp for it to bubble properly. The hinged lamp housing has a tendency to loosen with the vibration of train operation, thus allowing the bulb to drop away from the tube. Sealing the housing with friction tape solves the problem. Operator should pay attention to the wiring to the accessory's posts; the posts are close to an entry slot for the wires, and the wires must be carefully insulated to avoid a short circuit. However, it's all worth the trouble, for this massive accessory looks great on a layout. **Cross-references:** PW 455; ME 12848, 12902.

150   175

2306 OPERATING ICING STATION WITH CAR, 1982–83

Red roof, white chute, red-brown building structure, white upper building, sold with no. 6700 Southern Pacific refrigerator car. This accessory has become hard to find. Unlike LTI's later releases, this Fundimensions model is a direct reissue of the postwar version, complete with the original solenoid operation and the special Pacific Fruit Express refrigerator car. It shares the assets and liabilities of its predecessors. The solenoid moves the icing station's figure very fast, and the operating button must be pressed each time to activate the accessory. It is, however, a relatively trouble-free and clever accessory. It's still awkward to unload the ice cubes from the car once the accessory has been used. Instead of trying to keep the little swinging bin of the car open, try a large set of medical tongs to extract the cubes from the top. It saves wear on one's fingernails! Values include car. **Cross-references:** PW 352; ME 12703, 12847.

195   235

Exc   Mint

2315 COALING STATION, 1984–85

Dark red metal structure, gray support base, black pillars, red coal tray, gray roof. (Postwar version had maroon coal tray and green roof, and color of paint was a lighter red.) This reissue of a popular coal mover from the postwar years was originally scheduled for the number 2324, but in the chaos of the move to and from Mexico, production was delayed and that number was assigned to the Operating Switch Tower. When a hopper is parked under the accessory, which straddles the track, one push of a button dumps coal from an overhead bin. The coal gets there in the first place by being dumped into a trackside curved bin, which is then lifted by a string arrangement and dumped into the upper reservoir. This was a significant accessory because it used the newly developed sealed can motor instead of the big AC motor of the postwar version. The can motor is, of course, quieter and easier to maintain; it is also far less expensive to manufacture (though it is difficult to see how it could lift the same weight in plastic coal as its brawnier predecessor). As with the operating gantry crane, if the button is kept on for too long, the strings reverse on their spools and the button's "up" becomes "down." Otherwise the accessory has no surprises for the operator, except the usual spilled coal. **Cross-reference:** PW 497.

125   175

2316 NORFOLK & WESTERN OPERATING GANTRY CRANE, 1983–84

Dark maroon cab, gold lettering and cab base, maroon boom, gray superstructure. This remote-control gantry crane is essentially similar to the postwar 282R, but with a few important construction changes. It does not have the electromagnet found on the 282R, just an operating hook. This is a disadvantage because many times the hook is too light to extend the string downward when the operator wishes to lower the hook. If the line gets tangled in the process, the crane must be disassembled for rewinding of the line. If the lifting lever is left on for too long and the line gets to the top of its travel, the line reverses itself on its spool and lowers the load, reversing the sequence up-down on the control button. This is true of all Lionel gantry cranes. LTI's versions correct many of these problems by restoring the electromagnet. Also, the single motor and gearing of the 282R has been replaced by two can motors mounted under the superstructure, one for each operation of the crane (swiveling of body and hook operation). Compared to the 282R, this crane is not as strong a lifting device, but it operates more quietly than the 282R on much lower voltage. This first powered crane has been neglected since the Erie-Lackawanna magnetic version was issued, but it is somewhat scarce. **Cross-**

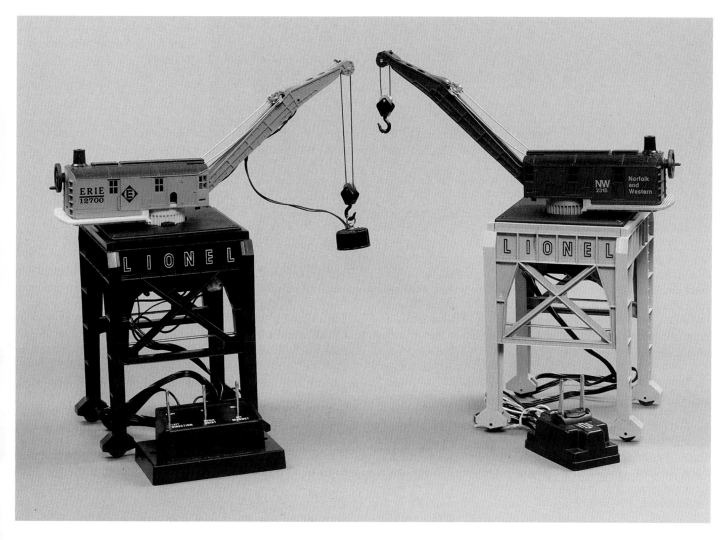

Left: The 12700 Erie-Lackawanna Magnetic Gantry Crane has escalated in value because it was offered for only one year and has a magnet. Right: The 2316 Norfolk & Western Operating Gantry Crane, which was cataloged in 1983 and 1984, was equipped with a hook and not a magnet.

	Exc	Mint
references: PW 282, 282R; ME 12700, 12834, 12922.	150	175

2321 OPERATING SAW MILL, 1984 and 1986–87

Dark red base, light tan house structures, dark green roofs, black metal lumber pickup mechanism, light tan fake sawdust pile, gray circular saw blade, yellow lumber cart. This was the second popular American Flyer accessory introduced by Fundimensions, and in many ways it is superior to Lionel's own lumber mill (though quite different in operation). When the accessory is activated, a lumber cart goes by a spinning saw blade, simulating cutting of the log. Then a finished lumber plank emerges from a compartment in a housing at the rear, where it is picked up by a lift mechanism and lifted

into a waiting trackside gondola or flatcar. The action is complex, colorful, and quaint. The new version makes use of the universal can motor, so it operates exceptionally smoothly. **Cross-reference:** PW Flyer 23796.

	Exc	Mint
	100	150

12700 ERIE-LACKAWANNA MAGNETIC GANTRY CRANE, 1987

Black gantry frame and platform with white-outlined "LIONEL", gray crane body and boom, yellow cab base and gear, maroon crane cab roof. LTI's production of Lionel accessories got off to a great start with this, the first modern-era gantry crane to revive the lift magnet of the postwar 282. Otherwise, it retained the drive system of the earlier Norfolk & Western magnetless model, with

The 12703 Icing Station brought back an old favorite in brighter colors.

Exc   Mint

two can motors, one for the turning cab and one for the hauling line. LTI designed the operating switch for this accessory in such a way that the lever activating the magnet must be held manually to keep it that way. In practice, this makes operation an exercise in fine motor skills, but at least it prevents one problem that bedeviled the postwar models: burned-out magnets caused by switches left in the "on" position. The magnet in this accessory does not seem as strong as those of its predecessors, but it can still lift a good load. Suggestion to operators: If you have an old piece of badly rusted track, cut it into 2" sections with a hacksaw for a realistic junk load. Production of this model was limited and, until the recent introduction of the Pennsylvania and New York Central models, it was in considerable demand. **Cross-references:** PW 282, 282R; ME 2316, 12834, 12922.

200   235

12701 DIESEL FUELING STATION, 1987

Dark blue housing on gray base, gray roof, orange sand tower stand and pipe base, black piping, black sand tank with yellow "DIESEL SAND", light gray figure with pink-colored face. Most Lionel collectors and operators consider this accessory a very slow mover that isn't too interesting, but perhaps LTI knows differently, for it is now in its third reissue since 1987. When operators pull their diesel locomotive up to the accessory, a press of a button moves a man from a trackside house to the side of the diesel with a fuel hose. The accessory has a large flywheel inside the house for smoother operation, and it works very well. **Cross-references:** PW 415, ME 12835, 12877.

100   125

12703 ICING STATION, 1988–89

Very bright orange housing, chutes and steps, red roof, dark gray superstructure with white lettering, black stamped steel base. Includes eight little ice cubes,

as do the special separate-sale refrigerator cars. This version of the icing station was changed significantly from both its postwar and modern-era predecessors. Instead of the solenoid-operated mechanism, it uses a can motor and a gear system to produce a much smoother operation. This accessory was sold without the special car, which has been available separately decorated for the New York Central, Reading, Great Northern, Virginian, and Burlington. Both this accessory and the cars have sold very well, although some collectors have complained about the extremely bright colors of this version. Operationally, one problem does occur: Sometimes the mechanism will not allow the paddleman to go back far enough to let the next ice cube drop from the chute. This can cause him to jam against the cube, sometimes losing his "arms"! Solution: Cut ⅛" off the paddle blade; even if the blade looks a little truncated, you'll have no further problem. See also 2306 for a somewhat bizarre solution to getting the ice cubes out of the operating car more efficiently. With its new smoothness, this accessory is a crowd-pleaser and a lot of fun to operate. **Cross-references:** PW 352; ME 2306, 12847.

90   120

12741 UNION PACIFIC MI-JACK INTERMODAL CRANE, 1989–90

Very large yellow crane structure with black Mi-Jack lettering and red, white, and blue Union Pacific shield logo, black simulated spotlights atop crane structure. This very modern accessory, the largest one produced by Lionel to that time, created quite a sensation when it was introduced. It signified LTI's commitment to move Lionel railroading into the truly modern freight-hauling age. Operationally, the accessory is awesome. This crane is capable of its own forward and reverse motion; it will also swing right or left, and its carrying jaws will open and shut, grasp a trailer, lift it (Lionel recommends lifting no more than seven ounces) and move it right or left. All this action is accomplished by a complex arrangement of string-driven motions powered by two can

Exc   Mint

motors mounted within a rooftop structure. The device works through a five-lever controller whose levers can work either singly or in combination. Lionel also supplied a 12-page instruction book with an impressively written history of the prototype. Both this and a second Norfolk & Western model have been heavily discounted because the accessory is too large for most home layouts. However, this accessory represents an ambitious new direction into modernity for Lionel, and it works well, providing operators with considerable entertainment. It is not, however, the first intermodal crane produced for a model railroad. That honor belongs to Cox Model Company, which made one in HO scale in the early 1970s. **Cross-reference:** ME 12781.

200   240

12781 NORFOLK & WESTERN INTERMODAL CRANE, 1990–91

Bright yellow crane structure, black "NW" logo, black simulated spotlights atop structure. Identical in function and appearance to 12741 Union Pacific model except for black "NW" lettering and logo on sides of superstructure. See 12741 for full operating details. There is one other distinction to this model; unlike the earlier Union Pacific version, this one has a lighted operator's cab along the right side. **Cross-reference:** ME 12741.

200   240

12798 FORK LIFT LOADER STATION, 1992–96

Light gray base, white building with red and white "LIONELVILLE" and "LIONELVILLE PIPE CO." signs, brown roof, orange, yellow, and black forklift truck, white simulated pipes beneath truck. This all-new accessory, made for LTI's Traditional Line, provides a relatively inexpensive yet massive device for a layout. At trackside, operators bring a double-door boxcar up to the accessory. When the button is pressed, a little lift truck comes out of the Lionelville Pipe Co. warehouse and appears to load a wedge of pipes into the car. In reality, the pipes stick out from the lift truck and a barrier at the edge of the truck's travel pushes them out of sight back under the truck. Then the lift truck goes back into the house, the pipes are pushed out again, and the process repeats. Simple and clever! The accessory is powered by a can motor. Some simple assembly is required.   **CP**

12834 PENNSYLVANIA GANTRY CRANE, 1993

Gray gantry structure, maroon cab (Whatever happened to good old Pennsylvania Tuscan red?), black boom and magnet casing, white road name, keystone herald, and numbers on cab. Except for its new road name and colors, this operating crane is identical to

Exc   Mint

the Erie-Lackawanna model. See 12700 for operating comments. **Cross-references:** PW 282, 282R; ME 2316, 12700, 12922.

135   150

12835 ILLUMINATED FUELING STATION, 1993

Dark chocolate brown base and roof, light tan house structure with brown window inserts and frosted windows, black and gray boom structure, blue attendant with white face and hands, dark blue sand tower structure with "DIESEL SAND" in yellow. Identical to 12701, except for new colors. See 12701 for comments. **Cross-references:** PW 415; ME 12701, 12877.

80   100

12847 OPERATING ICING STATION, 1994–95

Red-brown base structure with black metal base, light tan house, steps and chutes, green roof, solid blue figure with white paddles, comes with eight ice cubes. Identical to 12703 in operation, it has new and more subdued colors. See 12703 for operating comments. **Cross-references:** PW 352; ME 2306, 12703.

80   100

12848 OPERATING OIL DERRICK, 1994

Dark gray metal base, solid red derrick structure, white "LIONEL" signboards on derrick, black pumping structure, tube base and drum tray, red generator and rocking boom. Identical to 2305, except for new color scheme and signs. See 2305 for operating comments. **Cross-references:** PW 455; ME 2305, 12902.

100   135

12862 OPERATING OIL DRUM LOADER, 1994–95

Dark gray base and barrel ramp, yellow house with brown window and door outlines, green roof, orange lift truck, six metal barrels, black twin-light pole at one corner of base. Identical in operation to 2300, except for new color scheme and notable addition of a black twin lighting pole atop the far end of the base. See 2300 for operating comments. **Cross-references:** PW Flyer 779; ME 2300.

100   120

12873 OPERATING SAW MILL, 1995–97

Red-brown base, platforms and roof, white housing structure with frosted windows lettered "LIONEL SAW MILL", red "Main Office" door, red sawdust

The 12741 Union Pacific Mi-Jack Intermodal Crane caught the attention of operators and collectors alike when Lionel Trains Inc. introduced this large and exciting accessory in 1989.

	Exc	Mint

collector on roof. Comes with five varnished logs and five wood planks. Essentially identical to 2301 in operation; differs in color scheme. See 2301 for operating comments. **Cross-references:** PW 464; ME 2301.

                              100   **120**

12877 ILLUMINATED FUELING STATION, 1995

Black base and roof, dark red housing structure with red and black "LIONEL" sign and logo on side, black and gray boom structure, gray and yellow sand tower, frosted window inserts. Essentially identical to

Lionel enthusiasts looking for something new were delighted by the 12798 Fork Lift Loader Station when it was first cataloged in 1992.

	Exc	Mint

12701 and 12835 in operation; differs only in color scheme. See 12701 for operating comments. **Cross-references:** PW 415; ME 12701, 12835.

	75	90

12902 OPERATING MARATHON OIL DERRICK, 1995

Bright blue base, gray structure, red, white, and blue Marathon signs, black pumping apparatus and base, yellow generator and grasshopper pump arm. This version of the operating oil derrick is identical to its predecessors except for its color scheme, which is quite attractive. After the production of this accessory had begun, LTI apparently had a licensing problem with the oil company; as a result, no examples of this version will be manufactured other than those produced already. (This information came in a letter to Lionel

	Exc	Mint

Value-Added Dealers dated June 26, 1995. The same letter alludes to a no. 12930 "Lionelville" oil derrick to be produced during 1996.) The sudden cessation of production of the Marathon version should make it desirable to collectors; presumably its value will rise quickly. **Cross-references:** PW 455; ME 2305, 12848.

	150	195

12912 OIL PUMPING STATION, 1995–97

Maroon metal base with aluminized foil ID sign, black arm rocker structure, white generator and pump arm, gray pumping casing, pipe base and barrel tray. With this accessory, LTI did something useful and clever. It adapted the oil derrick into what is essentially a pump station without the derrick; the catalog even shows a base with the slots where the derrick would be fastened! In all other respects it operates in

Operating oil derricks have been integral parts of Lionel's modern-era line since the 2305 (right), wearing a Getty Oil Products sign, came out in 1981. The 12902 (left) carries on this tradition, though it advertises Marathon.

	Exc	Mint

the same way as the full derricks, but it is less expensive and adapts well to an operator's tank farm.

75   90

12915 LOG LOADER, 1996–97

Bright red unpainted plastic roof with large gray plastic finials, yellow unpainted roof supports, black log and motor shields, yellow unpainted plastic log bin and bright green unpainted plastic base. This reissue of the 164 accessory was eagerly awaited by operators and collectors; although it operates quite well, its appearance has disappointed some collectors. Most of the metal structure on the old 164 has been replaced by plastic, such as the black shield around the motor structure. As before, logs dumped into a tray are picked up by a chain hoist system and placed in a tray on the other

	Exc	Mint

side of the accessory, where a touch of a button dumps them into another car on an adjacent track. **Cross-reference:** PW 164.

CP

12916 WATER TANK, 1996–97

Red unpainted roof, light brown ("café-au-lait") tank with original Lionel markings, black tower support structure, dark gray die-cast base with two wire clips mounted on the underside, as on the 138 model. This long-awaited reissue of Lionel's most famous water tank features a few surprises for the operator. In appearance, it does have the heavy metal base, as advertised, but in all other respects it most closely resembles the watered-down 138 of later postwar years. This is evident from the roof, which fastens onto the tank top without the acorn-shaped nuts used on earlier versions and illustrated in the new Lionel catalog. Unlike its predecessors, the tank is not equipped with a solenoid to make the spout descend and rise. Instead, there is a new gear mechanism enclosed in a white plastic case and powered by a can motor. Time will tell if this arrangement has the durability of the old solenoids, but the mechanism produces a smooth descent of the spout instead of the hurried fall of the older versions. This mechanism was first used on the 12917 Operating Switch Tower, a reissue of the postwar 445. Apparently Lionel LLC intends to use this mechanism in all solenoid applications, since it is less expensive to manufacture. Like the switch tower, this accessory is made in China. **Cross-references:** PW 30, 138. **CP**

12922 NEW YORK CENTRAL OPERATING GANTRY CRANE, 1996

Dark gray gantry structure, black metal gantry base, Penn Central green cab with black roof, Penn Central green boom, black and white New York Central oval herald on cab, includes two black coil covers with white NYC logos. Identical in operation to 2316; it differs in road name and color scheme. This model does not have the operating magnet. See 2316 for operating comments. **Cross-references:** PW 282, 282R; ME 2316, 12700, 12834.

100   120

12929 OPERATING RAIL-TRUCK LOADING DOCK, 1996–97

Dark gray plastic roof and platform structure with light gray beams and supports; white lettering "LIONELVILLE RAIL/TRUCK TRANSFER DEPOT" on gray sign below roof. This new building kit is meant to straddle a wayside siding for unloading of boxcars onto road vehicles. At the press of a button, a worker trundles a barrel on a lift truck from the front to the back of the platform, giving the illusion of unloading the boxcar. This is essentially similar in operation (but in not appearance) to the 12798 Fork Lift Unloading Platform of 1992, except that it does not have the building structure. **Cross-reference:** ME 12798. **CP**

12930 LIONELVILLE OIL DERRICK, 1996

Blue-painted metal base, gray derrick structure, red generator and walking arm, white derrick signs with circle-L logo and "LIONELVILLE OIL CO." markings. This is the replacement for the suddenly canceled 12902 Marathon Oil Derrick, which ran into licensing difficulties. Incredibly, it is the third LTI reissue of the postwar 455 and the fourth modern-era remake (not to mention the 12912 Oil Pumping Station, which is essentially the

oil derrick platform without the derrick). This accessory is similar to the 12848, except for different colors. **Cross-references:** PW 455; ME 2305, 12848, 12902.
100   120

12936 SOUTHERN PACIFIC INTERMODAL CRANE, 1997

Yellow plastic framework, body and lift mechanism, black and gray simulated searchlights atop girders, large black rolling tires, Southern Pacific logo and Mi-Jack name atop superstructure in black. For 1997 Lionel LLC plans to reintroduce the massive Mi-Jack intermodal crane of 1988, and apparently it will operate as those earlier units do, with full forward-back, left-right and raise-lower functions controlled by a five-lever control center. The only discernible difference will be that the operator shack will be illuminated, as was the earlier Norfolk & Western model but not the first Union Pacific example. Some care is necessary to keep the operating strings properly aligned, but this big accessory works well. **Cross-references:** ME 12741, 12781, 12937. **CP**

12937 NORFOLK SOUTHERN INTERMODAL CRANE, 1997

Yellow plastic framework, body and lift mechanism, black and gray simulated searchlights atop girders, large black rolling tires, Norfolk Southern logo and Mi-Jack name atop superstructure in black. For 1997 Lionel LLC plans to reintroduce the massive Mi-Jack intermodal crane of 1988, and apparently it will operate as those earlier units do, with full forward-back, left-right and raise-lower functions controlled by a five-lever control center. **Cross-references:** ME 12741, 12781, 12936. **CP**

12958 INDUSTRIAL WATER TOWER, 1997

Catalog shows light gray base, green shack, red painted metal tower structure, silver tower top and base, and red blinking light at tower top. This accessory is being reissued for the first time since its postwar days. Although the production model may differ, the catalog for 1997 shows this tower in its most common postwar colors. The advertising copy states that the tower will have a blinking light at its top, as did the postwar version, but postwar Lionel had considerable trouble with its thermostatically controlled lamps. Most likely, the new tower will feature a diode-controlled on-off device similar to that found on the newer crossing signals. It would be much more reliable than a heat-controlled thermostat. **Cross-reference:** PW 193. **CP**

3

LIGHTING DEVICES

Well, yes, I could tell you of rail yards—
Iron crashes crying out in the night,
Soft green and red eyes of the switch lamps,
The stark spider webs of the yard tracks,
The hollow songs the wheel flanges make
When they whine around curves, hiss and thump
Of air compressors fighting to feed
Stiff brakes, angry dragon snorts
And growls of yard locomotives
Making up trains for morning runs
And the kerosene lamps of the old cabooses
Waiting, crude houses on wheels.

—from the author's "Your Railyard Vision"

INTRODUCTION

You remember what it was like, don't you? All you baby boom readers and perhaps those a little older . . . Don't you remember those days when you were running your train sets in your basements or attics and, when you got everything going, you went straight to the wall switch and turned out the room lights? Now, why would you do something strange like that?

You know the answer. . . . You wanted a "night scene" on your layout for all those lights! You and your friends would stand there in the soft red, green, and white glow of all those little lights on the trains, the switches, the transformer, the controllers, and especially where the little streetlights and interior lights of the accessories and houses shone. There was a magic to scenes like that, and they formed a happy part of many a childhood.

Fundimensions and Lionel Trains Inc. certainly remembered the allure of scenes like that. From the very

first days of the modern era, Fundimensions sought to bring life to its accessories through lights. The variety of these lighting accessories has always been formidable in Lionel's history, and the modern era would be no exception. If you didn't care for street scenes, you certainly had to care about the welfare of your busy industries. Perhaps you illuminated them with the bright eight-bulb Floodlight Tower, or maybe the twin Searchlight Tower a little later. Maybe the subtly blinking Microwave Relay Tower or the red and green Rotary Beacon were more to your taste. Or, like many, maybe you wanted them all, and the more lights on your layout, the better! Your advertising needs would be well represented by a Blinking Billboard, and perhaps the sides of your stations were graced by a brace of stately Goose Neck Street Lamps. One way or another, you'd find a way to light things up!

In 1970 Fundimensions began the parade of lights with the reissue of the old no. 76 Street Lamps, simple to send to the market quickly and crafted of plastic to be inexpensive. In fact, it wasn't unusual to find one, two, or even all three lamps packed into the 2170's box to be leftover postwar units. These darker green lampposts were also made with the MPC logo of the first three years of the modern era, but they soon gave way to a brighter green variety. Examples of these street lamps have even been found where postwar and MPC parts have been combined in both shades of green! The lamps themselves changed, too, from the clear push-pin L19 of the postwar years to a small screw-base bulb peculiar to the modern-era examples.

The street lamps weren't the only revivals of great interest. In those first few years of Fundimensions production, some very interesting—and scarce—revivals of the postwar floodlight and microwave towers were produced. As with the streetlights, some hybrid

Exc Mint

examples have been found. Of the six scarcest modern-era accessories of the early years, three are lighting devices covered in this chapter.

In recent years LTI introduced some more modern lighting accessories. A modernistic, round-globe set of lampposts produced a few years ago met with a cool reception, so LTI revived the 2170 model, this time in a handsome gray. An entirely new set of boulevard lights, sleek, slender, and modern, has emerged, and they have been used as illuminating devices for some of the modern era's best accessories, such as the third version of the Roadside Diner With Smoke. A new chrome-plated plastic double lamp has been mounted on some of the newer accessories, such as the second revival of the American Flyer Oil Drum Loader and the awesome Steam Clean and Wheel Grinding Shop. It should be only a matter of time before that lamp is sold as a separate item to update older accessories; it acts like a spotlight for the accessory's action. (Shades of the first 397 Operating Diesel-Type Coal Loader that was equipped with a no. 70 Yard Light!)

Just remember, railroaders: It's certainly no crime to keep a good old dream alive and revive memories of long-ago childhood days. It's even a better virtue to re-create those times with a whole new generation of young people ready to appreciate a little miniature magic. So set up that layout, turn on the power, and light it all up!

2170 STREET LAMPS, 1970–87

Lampposts sold three to a package, earliest versions carry postwar stamping on the underside of their bases but are packaged in Type I shrink-wrap or Type I boxes, later ones have Lionel MPC markings; they come in Type I, II, or III boxes. The numerous varieties listed below show how Fundimensions was trying to be efficient and use its inventory of parts. A bewildering variety of these otherwise mundane street lamps beckons the specialist collector. Although this little lamppost was produced in profusion and is certainly common, it presents quite a challenge to collect all its early varieties, which are indeed scarce because they were produced for such a short time. The earlier ones with L19 bulbs also shine a bit better than their successors. **Cross-references:** PW 76, ME 12874.

(A) 1970, dark green pole, dark green pole top, cream globe, pin-type bulbs; same bulb was used for postwar 76 Lamp Post.

20 25

(B) 1971, early; light green pole, mismatched dark green pole top, white globe, small foreign-made midget

Exc Mint

bulb with screw base. Note that a midget lamp is any lamp ¼" or less in diameter.

20 25

(C) 1971, later; Type I box dated 1971, lamps with light green base, pole, and cap base, translucent white globes, embossed on bottom "MADE IN U.S.A. / LIONEL MPC / MT. CLEMENS / MICH." MPC logo on top part of base, hand-etched 76-3 part number on bottom, foreign-made 8010-24 subminiature screw-base bulb.

20 25

(D) 1972–87, light green pole and pole top, white globe, midget screw-base bulb, Type II shrink-wrap packaging (earlier), Type II or Type III box (later).

15 20

2171 GOOSE NECK LAMPS, 1980–83

Lampposts sold as set of two in a Type III box, they have black plastic base and lamp structure mounted to metal pole and frosted pin-base bulbs. The postwar version of these lamps has been a nice prize for collectors of lampposts, and it's no surprise that the Fundimensions and LTI equivalents have their appeal as well. From the base a metal shaft rises and culminates in a gracefully curved filigreed piece to hold the lamp hood and lamp itself. The fixture looks much like the magnificent no. 58 of the prewar and early postwar years, and in the real world it looks like the fancy street lamps used on boulevards around the turn of the twentieth century. The hood pieces have served double duty for LTI as the attachment points for the lamps in the newer Illuminated Station Platforms. **Cross-references:** PW 75; ME 12742.

20 30

2195 FLOODLIGHT TOWER, 1970–72

Eight lights, metal light bracket and reflectors, takes older two-pin clear bulbs, tan base, "LIONEL" on two tabs near top of tower, transitional hybrid; unpainted gray plastic tower structure with unpainted gray "LIONEL" signs (postwar version has silver-painted tower structure, red-painted "LIONEL"), postwar microwave relay top on tower, postwar markings on base, Type I box. This early reissue of the postwar 195 accessory is one of the scarcest of the modern era. In fact, incredible as this may sound, this and a few other early modern-era accessories are scarcer than *any* regular-production postwar accessory, even the early 397 Operating Diesel-Type Coal Loader with a yellow generator cover and a yard light. Why would this be so? It is important to remember that when General Mills licensed the right to make Lionel trains

Both of the Fundimensions revivals of the postwar floodlight tower are becoming more difficult to find. The 2195 (left) was among the first accessories available in 1970. The 2313, with its handsome red plastic tower, was added to the line in 1975.

Exc   Mint

in late 1969, the marketplace for toy trains had deteriorated very badly. Therefore, in those early years while Lionel's new licensees tried to build up the market, the audience for Lionel's products was at an all-time low. Production, of course, was made to match the existing audience. In addition, many of these early accessories were cobbled together out of leftover parts, and the supply of these parts was limited. With these accessories, Fundimensions bought time to introduce its own new designs. The 2195 Floodlight Tower was almost—but not quite—identical to the postwar 195. It's probable that, in the absence of the Type I box, many collectors pass over this early design because it so closely resembles the very common 195. The gray of the tower structure is a shade darker on the Fundi-

mensions product, and though the "LIONEL" lettering is still on the tower structure, it is not painted red as on its predecessor. This hard-to-find accessory is a prize for collectors, especially in its Type I "Banner" box. **Cross-references:** PW 195; ME 2313, 12759.

55   **75**

2199 MICROWAVE TOWER, 1972–75

Black plastic base, unpainted dark gray plastic tower, black plastic top with three operating blinking light tips, postwar markings on base, Type II box. Although this accessory was produced later than the scarcer early Fundimensions ones, it is just as difficult

The 2199 Microwave Tower (right) has become somewhat difficult to find. More common is the 12723 (left), which Lionel Trains Inc. brought out in 1988.

	Exc	Mint

to find, perhaps even more so. It uses the same rubberized socket and pigtail-wired thermostat bulb as its 199 predecessor and, like the 2195, features a tower structure that has a significantly darker shade of gray. The "LIONEL" plates on the side of the tower are not painted red. The radar dishes are different as well; the postwar 199 has somewhat brittle white plastic dishes, while this version has more flexible translucent plastic radar dishes. **Cross-references:** PW 199; ME 12723.

70   90

2307 BILLBOARD LIGHT, 1982–86

Black die-cast post, hooded black metal light casting; attaches to base of billboard and blinks by thermo-

static control. This accessory was a revival of the postwar 410; even the original thermostat device was used. As packaged, it came with a light green billboard frame and one of the newer Fundimensions billboards, usually the Lionel one with the Santa Fe F3 diesels. (As labor leader John L. Lewis once said, "He who tooteth not his own horn, the same shall not be tooteth!") **Cross-references:** PW 410; ME 12882.

20   25

2313 ILLUMINATED FLOODLIGHT TOWER, 1975–83

Black plastic base, red plastic tower, black plastic top, gray light bar, eight miniature lights, two binding posts on bottom. As Fundimensions brought out modified designs of postwar accessories (as opposed to direct reissues), things got "curiouser and curiouser" in the Lionel accessory world. The 2195 was essentially a reissued 195, but the 2313 showed substantial modification from the original design, especially with the floodlight bar atop the tower. The postwar light bar has a metal frame running around its rear that provides contact for the lights; beginning with this version, the metal frame is absent and two wires come down from the mounting holes of the light bar to make electrical contact and carry power internally to the bulbs. The bulbs were no longer the L-19 push-pin type; instead, they were a newly designed type with a white base with pigtail wires designed to plug into a white nylon socket. At first the bulbs were small round ones; later, the globes became elongated. This is not so much a design change as a shift to a different outside contractor. Metal lamp shades were used at first, probably from a leftover quantity of parts. Later production had chromed plastic shades, the practice through the 12759. **Cross-references:** PW 195; ME 2195, 12759.

A) Early hybrid, takes miniature plastic-base lamps, but reflectors remain metal. This version has the later light bar; came in Type II box with "GAUGE" misspelled as "GUAGE" on front label. In view of its unusual nature, this version is surprisingly common.

30   40

(B) Same as (A), but regular production, light reflectors are chromed plastic instead of metal. "GAUGE" is spelled correctly on box.

25   30

2314 ILLUMINATED SEARCHLIGHT TOWER, 1975–83

This accessory was a new and clever (if somewhat fragile) adaptation of older designs of parts to form something different. From the tower base to the metal rods for electrical contact, the accessory resembles the 2313 Floodlight Tower. However, two large searchlights made from the old mold for the postwar searchlight car have been fitted with special brackets to attach them to the metal rods. These lights can swivel and tilt, but they are really fragile, especially the brackets. The light socket is the newer nylon-base type, and inside the searchlight casing there is a chromed plastic reflector. There are also several scarce versions of this accessory. In 1975 it was pictured in the catalog in an all-gray version, but so far the existence of this piece has been highly questionable. (If you have one known to be original, please enlighten us!) The 2314 does exist in an all-black version that is difficult to

find. The most common version has a red tower and top. **Cross-references:** ME 12716, 12899.

(A) Unpainted light gray plastic tower and dark gray base, two black searchlight hoods; rare. Shown in 1975–77 catalogs; reader confirmation of these colors requested. **NRS**

(B) Black plastic tower, base, and tower top, two black searchlight hoods. Somewhat hard to find.

40   50

(C) Same as (A), but red tower and top, black base; common variety.

20   30

(D) Same as (C), but black tower top; interesting variation because it shows a clear progression from all-black version to the common red one.

30   40

2494 ROTARY BEACON, 1972–74

Red sheet-metal tower with revolving beacon powered by vibrator motor, beacon projects red and green illumination, over 11½" high, red stamped metal base 5" x 5"; black ladder, black-lettered aluminized foil nameplate on base, two clips on underside of base for wires. This early accessory has gotten some attention lately because of the reissue by LTI of two new versions that closely parallel postwar 494. However, there is a major construction difference between this Fundimensions reissue and those of LTI. True to its 494 heritage, the 2494 still has a metal rod (in this case black) connecting the base to the tower top inside the structure. This rod serves as one of the electrical contacts. In the LTI versions, this rod is absent. Instead, one corner of the structure has been equipped with little tabs to hold two (instead of one) wires from the clips to the tower top. The construction of the light hood differs from that on the 494; a black plastic light hood rotates on circular metal collar that often is missing from used examples. The box was made by the Stone Container Corp.; some examples have a glued-on paper overlay with a black and white picture of the accessory, others do not. This is one of the scarcest of all the Fundimensions accessories. Some versions are known to have been issued with leftover postwar beacon tops instead of new assemblies. This poses a problem of authenticity for buyers. The postwar top is common, while the 2494 top is scarce. Since the LTI versions use the same rotating top, how can collectors tell if they have an original 2494 top? Look carefully at the lenses in the assembly. On the real 2494 rotating top, the green and red lenses are very pale; the red lens even looks as if it has a pinkish cast to it. On the LTI versions, the green and red lenses are much brighter

Fundimensions created the 2314 Illuminated Searchlight Tower in 1975 by adapting older designs of parts. Version B (right) features a black tower and top, while version D (left) has a red tower and black top.

Exc   Mint

in color—a true shade of green and red. The top with the pale lenses is the only genuine 2494 top. **Cross-references:** PW 494; ME 12720, 12831.

(A) Postwar 494 silver beacon heads; does not include metal collar because it is not necessary for this beacon top.

50   60

(B) Black beacon head with pale red and green lenses; see description above. Includes unpainted metal collar, which surrounds vibrator motor insulation. (Later LTI metal collars are black.)

60   75

12708 STREET LAMPS, 1988–91

Sold in sets of three, each lamp has black base and pole, white opaque rounded globe atop pole. These were an attempt to modernize Lionel's lamp designs and still provide operators with low-cost lampposts. They were not, as a rule, well received. The problem

Exc   Mint

was their translucent nylon globes, which had a rubbery feel to them and did not show light very well. The accessory used a subminiature screw-base bulb similar to those used on HO lampposts, which perhaps was another problem to some operators.

10   15

12716 SEARCHLIGHT TOWER, 1987–91

Light gray base and tower platform, bright orange tower structure, black searchlight hoods. This was the first LTI version of the twin searchlight tower. It was identical to the late design except for its colors. The lamps were of the elongated nylon socket and base type. **Cross-references:** ME 2314, 12899.

25   30

12720 ROTARY BEACON, 1988–89

Red base and tower structure, aluminized foil identification plate on base, black tower top, black metal

Street lamps are essential parts of any model railroad, and the Lionel line has included them since the prewar era. First to appear in the modern era was the 2170 (left), based directly on a postwar design. The 12708 (center), introduced in 1988, represented something new and up-to-date. Six years later, Lionel Trains offered another new model, the 12804 Highway Lights (right), which proved to be very popular.

	Exc	Mint

vibrator motor collar, black plastic rotating top with bright green and red lenses uses bayonet-base 14-volt bulb. Refer to the 2494 for a complete discussion about the construction differences between this first LTI version and the scarce Fundimensions model. Briefly, the metal rod of the earlier versions has been replaced by two wires and the rotating beacon top has subtle differences in the shading of the lens. The tower top is black instead of the all-red of the 2494, and the metal collar is black and not unpainted metal. **Cross-references:** PW 494; ME 2494, 12831.

50   70

12723 MICROWAVE RELAY TOWER, 1988–91 and 1994

Dark gray base, bright orange tower structure, white radar dish (neither brittle nor translucent), light blinks thermostatically. This LTI reissue uses the same operating structure, but the colors are much brighter, as is true with many of LTI's first accessories.

	Exc	Mint

These brighter color schemes are no accident. In the prewar years, Joshua Lionel Cowen insisted on rich enameled colors for Lionel's rolling stock and accessories, even at the cost of some realism, because he knew bright colors attracted women, who then (as now) had a major voice in the selection of the holiday train set. LTI seems to have learned that wisdom, and these brighter colors exude an attitude of optimism on the part of the firm—a welcome note for collectors and operators. **Cross-references:** PW 199; ME 2199.

25   35

12742 GOOSE NECK STREET LAMPS, 1989–97

Sold in pairs, each lamp has black structure and base attached to metal rod, uses frosted pin bulb. This LTI reissue is identical to the earlier Fundimensions model; however, it uses a new frosted pin bulb, which gives a much softer illumination. **Cross-references:** PW 75; ME 2171.

25   35

12759 FLOODLIGHT TOWER, 1990–94

Light gray base and tower top, bright orange tower structure, chromed plastic reflectors, takes plastic-based lamps. This LTI tower is identical in construction to the late Fundimensions 2313; it uses chromed plastic reflectors and elongated nylon base and socket bulbs. **Cross-references:** PW 195; ME 2195, 2313.

25   35

12804 HIGHWAY LIGHTS, 1992–97

Sold in sets of four; each has light gray round base, gray slender pole bent at 45-degree angle, elongated gray lamp shade. This all-new LTI street light is not too different from similar models offered by other manufacturers and looks as fragile. It has also been used to illuminate such accessories as the third LTI Roadside Diner With Smoke. They are 6" high and use a new (for Lionel) clear tubular bulb that throws good illumination, thanks to the post's elongated shade. These lights give a modern look to city streets.

CP

12831 ROTARY BEACON, 1993–95

Silver-painted base and tower structure, black tower top, black metal vibrator motor collar, black plastic rotating beacon with bright red and green lenses. This version of the rotary beacon is the equivalent to the postwar silver 494. See 2494 and 12720 for construction details. **Cross-references:** PW 494; ME 2494, 12720.

40   60

Rotary beacons, with their red and green beams of light, give beauty and drama to a layout. The 2494 (left) was introduced in 1972 and cataloged through 1974. Next came the 12720 (center) in 1988 and 1989, followed by the silver 12831 in 1993. The latter remained in the line for two more years.

Exc Mint

12874 STREET LAMPS, 1994–97

Sold in sets of three, each lamp has dark gray plastic post and base, white translucent lamp cover. LTI brought back the original Lionel design of these street lamps for two good reasons. One was that the disappointing reception given its modernized design (see 12708). The second was to stay competitive with other manufacturers such as K-Line, which used old Marx dies to produce similar lampposts. This version uses a subminiature screw-base bulb. **Cross-references:** PW 76; ME 2170.

CP

12882 ILLUMINATED BILLBOARD, 1995–96

Black metal lamp bracket and lens hood with thermostat device; assembly clips to base of billboard; black billboard frame with white, red, and black "Lionel Visitors' Center" billboard. Identical to both 410 and 2307, except for slight differences in the fastening of the thermostat device to the lamp pole. Like its predecessors, this version uses a bayonet-base clear bulb and blinks on and off. This time the billboard frame is black, and the enclosed billboard advertises the Lionel Visitors' Center. However, any standard Lionel billboard fits the frame.

CP

12886 "395" FLOODLIGHT TOWER, 1995–97

Silver painted metal tower base and structure; aluminized foil identification plate on base, black tower top (immediate visual identification for this version), black lamp brackets and hoods. The reissue of the postwar 395 accessory has long been awaited by operators and collectors, and it finally has emerged. The postwar version was produced in yellow, red, painted silver, un-

painted aluminum, and 45N green (in order of scarcity). The construction differences follow those of the Rotary Beacon: the center rod is absent and has been replaced by two wires. However, the beautiful die-cast black brackets and lens hoods of the 395 have been retained. The wiring on this accessory has always been very sensitive, since it is wired in series and the ground contact for the bulbs is found at the juncture of the hood and its bracket. You may have to "play around" with the position of the lamp hoods to get them to work—just like veteran postwar operators!

CP

12899 SEARCHLIGHT TOWER, 1995–97

Dark brown plastic base, structure and top; black searchlight hoods; uses elongated nylon socket and base bulb, chromed reflectors inside searchlight hoods. Structurally identical to earlier 12716. **Cross-references:** ME 2314, 12716.

CP

12927 YARD LIGHT, 1996–97

Black plastic pole, base, and lamp hood, chromed lamp reflectors. Two lamps mounted side by side at top of pole. This new twin-light design made its debut earlier with the 12767 Steam Clean and Wheel Grinding Shop in 1992. There, it provided illumination for the various functions of that accessory. Apparently it also created a demand for a new yard light; as a result, Lionel now sells this twin light in sets of three. It is a somewhat fragile plastic piece that takes subminiature plug-in bulbs. The version sold separately has a flat bottom; the ones included with the 12767 accessory have two projecting pegs which plug into the accessory base.

CP

4

ROAD AND STREET CROSSING DEVICES

Fierce-throated beauty!
Roll through my chaunt with all thy lawless music,
thy swinging lamps at night,
Thy madly-whistled laughter, echoing, rumbling
like an earthquake, rousing all,
Law of thyself complete, thine own track firmly
holding . . .

—Walt Whitman, "To a Locomotive in Winter"

INTRODUCTION

You have to read it to believe it. Right there, in the 1935 catalog, in language usually reserved for Charlton Heston as Moses delivering the Ten Commandments, thunders "THE MOST UNUSUAL RAILROAD AC-CESSORY EVER CONCEIVED!" This Hollywoodian introduction presented to Lionel Land the Automatic Gateman, and for once the hype may have been right. This little accessory (with an occasional "vacation" recently) has been in the Lionel catalog ever since. Small wonder (in two senses of the phrase): The gateman was, and is, a charming accessory. Thousands of children have smiled and laughed at the little man coming out of his wayside shack with his diminutive red lantern to warn motorists of oncoming trains. Ironically, Lionel introduced this accessory just at the time when its real equivalent was being phased out rapidly by railroads, for another device — and its Lionel equivalent — was beginning its widespread use.

This device is, of course, the Automatic Crossing Gate. Although collectors and operators tend to take this accessory for granted because it has run in Lionel's inventory even longer than the Automatic Gateman, its story is perhaps even more amazing than

that of any other accessory. Lionel's very first version of the crossing gate, no. 77, was cataloged in 1923. The first actual crossing gate in use by American railroads was not installed until the following year! It was quite curious that Lionel could be so predictive with one accessory and reactive with another. However, this story proves that Lionel had its ear to the rail alertly in anticipating developments on the real railroads. Later, no sooner did the Chicago, Burlington & Quincy's *Zephyr* appear in 1934 than Lionel had its own miniature version produced for sale.

In one form or another, Lionel has produced all the major road and street crossing devices available to real railroads. Look at the catalogs for both the postwar and modern era, and you will see banjo signals, crossing gates of all stripes (literally), crossing gates with flashing signals, automatic highway flashers — the works! All of them work extremely well, and all of them add great charm and action to any layout.

In the first years of the modern era, Fundimensions found that it had quite a few postwar examples left in its inventory. These were marketed in new Type I "banner" boxes as long as the supply lasted, and now these examples are difficult to find. Some even came in bizarre forms and packaging. For example, collectors have ridiculed the absurd picture of the Highway Crossing Signal as portrayed in the 1971 catalog; the top piece of a 262 Crossing Gate And Signal is rammed into an elongated leftover postwar block signal base. Guess what? An authentic example of a similar configuration has been found! (See 2154 B below.) One example of the 2162 Crossing Gate And Signal has been found packed into a double-relettered postwar box. At first, the box was made for an 1122-100 switch; it was then relabeled for a 262 signal, and atop that is a little

The 2140 Automatic Banjo Signal (left) was introduced in 1970 and became a basic part of the Lionel line. By contrast, the 12729 Mail Pickup Set (right), another revival of a postwar accessory, wasn't added until 1988.

paste-on paper label with the number "2162"! These Frankensteinian combinations probably came from assemblies made using the last of the parts at the old Hillside, New Jersey, factory, which was producing a few items even after the move to Mount Clemens but before it closed in late 1972.

Operationally, these accessories are very reliable. However, the pressure-activated 141 and 153C Contactors demand constant readjustment, and, since the track must bend under the train's weight to activate them, they preclude much track ballasting for realism. The solution for this state of affairs is to bypass the contactors completely and use a section of insulated track to operate the accessory.

If an accessory has two contacts, just wire both to a track lockon fastened to the middle rail and the outside insulated rail. If it has three contacts for constant lighting, use two lockons, one on the insulated track and another on a live track. Hook the ground wire to the center rail and the wire to the lightbulb to the live regular track rail (or use constant-voltage posts of the transformer itself). Then hook the wire to the activating device to the insulated outside rail so the train itself triggers the accessory. Voilà!

Yes, these roadside crossing accessories have some interesting stories to tell us. However, the main reason to pay attention to them is their transcendent popularity with the public. These accessories always sold well, no matter what the economic or toy train climate. More than any other Lionel accessories, they reflected the familiar railroad world. No wonder it's so difficult to imagine a Lionel railroad of any kind without at least a few of them.

Exc   Mint

2128 AUTOMATIC SWITCHMAN, 1983–86

Gray-painted metal base with green cardboard bottom, red tanks, lumber stack of planks like those of the Operating Sawmill. This reissue of the slow-selling postwar 1047 may have been less expensive than its related Automatic Gateman, but part of the gateman's charm was that he popped out of a little shack. That does not happen here; the figure just stands on the platform and moves forward to wave a flag at the oncoming motorists or train. It also has a plastic crossbuck like the 2145, but its real progenitor is probably the prewar and postwar 1045 Operating Flagman, which was a lot more popular because the figure was so grotesquely oversized. Somehow this accessory just misses the mark, and it has never sold well. It is, however, prized by many collectors for its scarcity. This version came in a Type III box. **Cross-references:** PW 1047, ME 12892.

                                          35   45

2140 AUTOMATIC BANJO SIGNAL, 1970–83

Black metal base and pole, black plastic crossbuck with white lettering, black banjo sign with white lettering, bayonet-base red light. 7½" high. The swinging banjo signal has always been a popular operating accessory on tinplate railroads, right from the days of the magnificent one brought out by Ives. Lionel's version uses a little vibrator motor, which rotates a cylindrical eccentric cam. A notch in the banjo sign fits onto a projection of the cam, which allows the sign to wigwag back and forth to the accompaniment of a "peek-a-boo" red light. Manufacturing tolerances are wide for this accessory; some spin readily while others take considerable voltage to activate. The first modern-era versions of the 2140 were leftover 140 pieces packaged in Type I "Banner" boxes; these are quite hard to find. **Cross-references:** PW 140; ME 12709.

(A) "LIONEL CORPORATION" stamped on underside of base; postwar carryover. Came in Type I Fundimensions box.

                                          35   45

(B) Same as (A), but Type II box; accessory with postwar markings.

                                          30   35

(C) MPC logo on base, Type II Fundimensions box.

                                          30   35

The Lionel gateman, perhaps the most famous toy train accessory ever produced, has been going strong since 1935. The earliest modern-era version of the 2145 (left) came packaged in a box with a cellophane window that resembled the packaging given the 145 during the early 1960s (center). From 1973 through 1977, the 2145 Automatic Gateman came in a box that substituted a color photograph of the accessory.

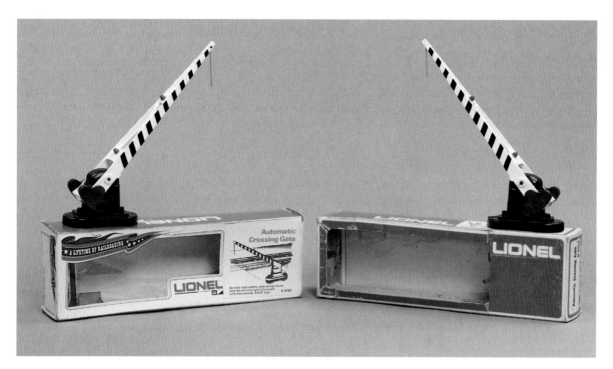

Fundimensions cataloged the 2152 Automatic Crossing Gate from 1972 through 1986 with different packaging. Version A came in a Type I box (left), and version B came in a Type II box (right).

2145 AUTOMATIC GATEMAN, 1972–84

Structured identically to postwar 145, with a few color changes, dark flat green base, white corrugated plastic shed, brown (sometimes closer to maroon) door, roof and window inserts, red and gold "LIONELVILLE" sign above the door, and unpainted figure with red lantern. The rather fragile white crossbuck warning sign attached to the base by a metal plate is also retained throughout the accessory's run. This accessory was first offered in 1935 as the 45 for Standard gauge and the 045 for O gauge (differing only in the size of special insulated track and the box size needed to accommodate it). In 1937 its number changed to 45N, signifying the use of a 41 Contactor instead of an insulated track, and in 1950 it was substantially revised and changed to the 145. Its spectacular market success reflects its great play value. The gateman, who is really a watchman, rushes from his lighted shed as the train approaches. He warns pedestrians and vehicles with his swinging lantern and returns to the shed after the train passes. The accessory came with a pressure contactor and a lockon.

There is some doubt about the first modern-era version of the 2145. A few collectors state that leftover 145 pieces were packaged into Type I "Banner" boxes with cello front windows, but the existence of this packaging has never been confirmed by photograph; confirmation would be welcomed. Given the early history of Fundimensions, such a version of the 2145 is certainly possible. The first authenticated version in the modern era is the 2145 issued in 1972. It featured a much darker green base than the 145 and darker brown roof and window inserts. It was packaged horizontally in a Type II window box, the only year this box was used. Then, without change to the accessory, the box became a Type II windowless variety that opened at the top, not the end. The only other key change came in 1978, when the configuration of the windows in the door changed from two large windows to twelve smaller ones. **Cross-references:** PW 145; ME 12713.

	Exc	Mint

(A) 1970–71, green metal base, white shed with brown door and window, frosted plastic window inserts, maroon roof and toolshed lid, must have Fundimensions Type I box; this accessory was a 145 in Fundimensions packaging. Confirmation by photograph is requested.

NRS

(B) 1972, brown roof and toolshed lid, darker green base, Type II rectangular box with window; accessory packed horizontally.

35   45

(C) 1973–75, same as (B), but packed in rectangular Type II box without window.

30   40

(D) 1976–84, medium light green base, white shack, maroon doors, windows, toolbox lid, and roof, Type III box. In 1978, door changes from two panes to twelve.

30   40

Exc   Mint

2152 AUTOMATIC CROSSING GATE, 1970–86

Black plastic base, white plastic gate with gray weights, on bottom "#252 Crossing Gate", came with 153C pressure contactor. The Fundimensions version can be distinguished from its 252 counterpart by the presence of a black plastic gate rest at the end of the gate arm rather than the metal one used in the postwar version. Many postwar examples were repacked into Fundimensions Type I and Type II boxes. Some examples were sold in Type III rolling stock boxes with black print; "6-2152 AUTOMATIC CROSSING GATE" on the ends. Structurally, the accessory was identical to 252. **Cross-references:** PW 252; ME 12714, 12888.

(A) Type I box; postwar leftover, has new MPC instruction sheet.   **30   40**

(B) Type II box; postwar leftover or (predominantly) Fundimensions production.

                                                        25   35

Exc   Mint

(C) Type III box in two varieties: rolling stock window box with paste-on labels or windowless box with much thicker cardstock and color photo of the gate.

                                                        25   35

2154 AUTOMATIC HIGHWAY FLASHER, 1970–87

Another venerable accessory, this item goes back to 1940 in Lionel's history. When a train contacts a special split-plate 154C Contactor that attaches to the top of the rail (rather Marx-like in operation), each light in the signal flashes in alternation. This device clamps over the track and has two thin metal plates, which are insulated from the rail. The flasher is wired so that train wheels run across the metal flanges, completing the circuit to each of the two bulbs in turn. Thus the left light goes on and off as the wheels pass over the left plate, and the right light goes on and off with the right plate, giving the flashing appearance. This clever contactor first appeared in 1940 with the initial versions of the 154. The later LTI versions do not use this

The Automatic Highway Flasher and its packaging have changed in noticeable ways during the modern era. The 2154 (center) was the first model, and it resembled the postwar version (left). Next came the 12760 and the 12888 (right), which featured a black crossbuck and a black finial cap.

Exc   Mint

contactor; instead, they have an electronic device inside the accessory that provides the flashing of the lights. The first versions marketed in the modern era are postwar leftovers with white crossbucks and black lettering; they are found in the Type I "Banner" box. Later versions in Type II and III boxes are Fundimensions production; they have black plastic crossbucks with white lettering. Modern-era production has been observed in several colors. Reader comments are needed with the specific examples. **Cross-references:** PW 154; ME 12760, 12888.

(A) White plastic crossbuck with raised black lettering, gray unpainted post with chrome finial cap; 154 packaged in a Type I Fundimensions box.

30   40

(B) Same as (A), except post is installed in black base from leftover 151 Semaphore. Verified from photographs. In the 1971 catalog, the 2154 is shown in the form of a 2162 top piece somehow installed into the base of a 2163 Block Signal. Other odd combinations of parts may exist; reader comments requested.

NRS

(C) Black crossbuck with raised white lettering, black finial cap, MPC logo stamped on underside of base.

25   35

(D) Black finial cap, white crossbuck, MPC logo on base, pink "STOP", Type II box. Unusual combination of postwar and MPC parts.

30   40

2162 AUTOMATIC CROSSING GATE AND SIGNAL, 1970–87, 1994, and 1996

Black plastic base, black crossbuck with white lettering and simulated bell at top, black or red stripes on white gate, red bulbs with pins, pressure contactor, lockon. This combined crossing gate and flashing signal ran for quite some time in both the postwar and the modern-era catalogs. There were many leftover pieces that were repackaged into Type I "Banner" boxes and other unorthodox packaging (see listings below). It is stamped on the underside: "NO. [blanked out] CROSSING GATE / MADE IN U.S. OF AMERICA / THE LIONEL CORPORATION, N.Y." The number 252 was deleted from the die when the base was reused for the 2162. The stripes on the gate can be black or red for either era, depending on the production run. (The 1996 Spring Release Catalogue shows red stripes.) As with the 2152 Crossing Gate, postwar examples have a metal support rod, while modern-era ones use plastic. During the latest run of the accessory in the early 1990s, the Type VI packing box seemed to

Exc   Mint

imply that the bulbs flashed because the picture of the accessory showed one bulb shining and the other unlit. This prompted complaints, since the accessory never operated that way; both lights came on and remained on. Several dealers had to relabel the boxes "Does Not Flash" to avoid confusion. It is also interesting that the accessory is now jumping into and out of the catalog after such a long absence. **Cross-reference:** PW 262.

(A) Red gate stripes, metal support rod; postwar leftover repackaged in a double-relabeled box originally meant for an 1122-100 027 switch. White box with orange lettering has orange and white paste-on label for 262 Crossing Gate And Signal, but plain paper paste-on label is applied atop the 262 number with black typed "#2162". Very unusual packaging, to say the least; gate had to be disassembled to fit into the box.

40   50

(B) Red-painted diagonal stripes, metal support rod on gate, Type I box, postwar markings on base, postwar carry-over in Fundimensions box.

25   35

(C) Same as (B), but black diagonal stripes instead of red.

25   35

(D) Same as (B), but black-painted diagonal stripes, black plastic support rod on gate, Type II box, postwar markings on base blanked out.

25   35

(E) Same as (D), but later production; diagonal stripes are red.

25   35

2309 MECHANICAL CROSSING GATE KIT, 1982–92

Black plastic track bracket, gate support and pole, white plastic gate, white crossbuck with black lettering; identical to the earlier 2310, but in kit form instead of preassembled. During its long run of production, this little plastic crossing gate was, it seemed, everywhere. It was available for separate sale, of course, but it was also to be found in many a starter train set. Although operators and collectors do not pay much attention to it, this gate was a noteworthy and successful attempt by Fundimensions to produce a truly inexpensive operating accessory. It operates by the weight of the train bending down a support that holds the gate upright, thus letting it fall. Later in production, the ready-made versions were changed into kits, which would explain the number changes. **Cross-reference:** ME 2310.

4   8

Versions C (left) and D (right) of the 2162 Automatic Crossing Gate and Signal, which entered the line in 1970 and was cataloged with only minor changes in appearance and packaging through 1987.

Fundimensions brought out the simple yet enjoyable 2309 Mechanical Crossing Gate Kit in 1982, and it remained in the Lionel line through 1992. The 2309 was a built-it-yourself version of the 2310 Mechanical Crossing Gate.

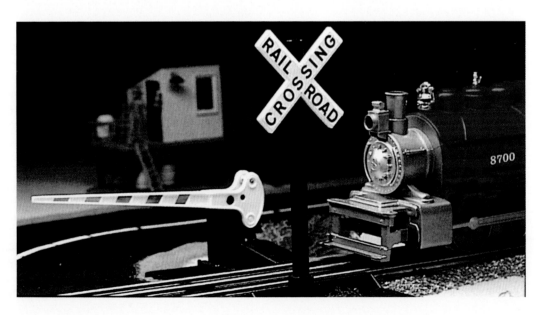

The automatic gateman lives on, its latest incarnation being the 12713 (left), which includes a gray figure in a yellow shack with a red roof. Next to it is the 2128 Automatic Switchman, a Fundimensions reissue of a postwar accessory.

	Exc	Mint

2310 MECHANICAL CROSSING GATE, 1973–77

Identical to later 2309, except that it came ready-made in Type III box instead of as a kit. **Cross-reference:** ME 2309.

	4	8

12709 OPERATING BANJO SIGNAL, 1987–91

Tuscan red-painted base and shaft, matching Tuscan crossbuck and signs with white lettering. Although this version of the banjo signal operated exactly the same as the 2140, it represented LTI's desire to introduce brighter colors into its accessories. **Cross-references:** PW 140; ME 2140.

	30	35

	Exc	Mint

12713 AUTOMATIC GATEMAN, 1987–88 and 1994–97

Light tan base, green cardboard base bottom (we would like to know if some earlier 2145 versions also have this base), doorstop bump designed into metal base, bright yellow shack, red roof and toolbox lid, light gray figure with red lantern, white crossbuck with black lettering and metal base. Still illuminated by 431 large-base bayonet bulb present with this accessory since 1950, but cardboard shield added to this version to prevent translucence. It reappeared in the LTI catalogs from time to time. This version is done in extremely bright colors; unfortunately, the plastic of this model is translucent enough to let light bleed through the walls, door, and roof. (A cardboard piece on the roof prevents light leakage there.) It has also been cheapened a bit by the addition of a cardstock base bottom instead of the sturdy galvanized metal ones of previous versions. However, it operates just as dependably as older versions. **Cross-references:** PW 145; ME 2145.

CP

12714 AUTOMATIC CROSSING GATE, 1987–91 and 1994–97

Gray base, red safety stripes, brown plastic gate stop rod. This version of the crossing gate is done in LTI's new and brighter colors. Otherwise it operates in the same fashion as previous versions. It has been packaged in both LTI's Type VI box, earlier in its pro-

duction, and later in a window-front orange Type V "collector" box. **Cross-references:** PW 252; ME 2152.

CP

12760 AUTOMATIC HIGHWAY FLASHER, 1990–91

Tuscan base and crossbuck with white lettering, silver painted pole with black finial cap, black die-cast light hood piece. This version of the twin-light highway flasher resembles its predecessors except for color, but its operation has been greatly improved by the inclusion of an electronic operating system. This enables operators to dispense with the old split-plate 154C Contactor in favor of a 153C pressure contactor or an insulated rail section. The lights flash more

The 12797 Crossing Gate and Signal, photographed for the 1991 Lionel Trains Inc. catalog, would have made a superb addition to the line. Unfortunately, it never went into mass-production, perhaps because projected sales did not meet expectations.

prototypically and steadily with this system. **Cross-references:** PW 154; ME 2154, 12888.

35   45

12797 CROSSING GATE AND SIGNAL, 1991

Catalog shows silver base and superstructure, white crossbuck with black lettering, white gate with red striping and two sets of flashing lights, each with one amber and one red lens. Accessory was to have warning bell when activated. This interesting-looking and modern crossing gate and signal was to resemble those produced in large scale by LGB and others that have two sets of flashing lights and a warning bell. It was never made, probably because it was not cost-effective enough to attract good projected sales.

Not manufactured

12839 GRADE CROSSING, 1993–97

Red-brown plastic one-piece double ramp designed to fit under a straight section of O or O27 gauge track to simulate grade crossing for roadway; sold in pairs; can be used alongside one another for multiple lanes. It took Lionel a long time to produce so simple an accessory as this, which is vital for layout builders.

CP

12888 RAILROAD CROSSING FLASHER, 1995–97

Black base, black crossbuck with white lettering, silver-painted pole with black finial cap, black die-cast light hood piece. Identical to the 12760, including new electronic operating mechanism, but in traditional colors of postwar and Fundimensions models. The lamps in this version have been changed from the red bayonet-base type to the small plug-in red pin type. Many operators think this change detracts from the 12888, though it obviously reduces the per-unit cost. **Cross-references:** PW 154; ME 2154, 12760.

CP

12892 AUTOMATIC FLAGMAN, 1995–97

Black-painted metal base, red tanks, unvarnished lumber planks on rack, white plastic crossbuck sign with die-cast base (same as 145 Automatic Gateman and successors, and just as fragile), hand-painted flagman figure with blue uniform, white shirt, pink face and hands, and red flag. This version of the accessory is identical to the 2128, but now it has more dramatic and attractive colors. As before, when the accessory is activated, the hand-painted figure steps forward to wave his warning flag. **Cross-references:** PW 1047; ME 2128.

CP

5

TRACKSIDE SIGNAL DEVICES

What would a railroader of a later time think of running over an unlighted single track, upon a dark and gloomy night, with a "doubleheader" . . . loaded with troops, horses, cannon . . . ammunition and accouterments, with the old-fashioned car platforms, loose-couples, at a speed of 40 MPH, with neither a train brake, a signal cord, a semaphore or a mast signal at a station? And yet this was common practice in Civil War times.
— Bill Yenne, Ed., *The Romance and Folklore of North America's Railroads*

INTRODUCTION

The trouble with trains is they just don't stop on the proverbial dime. It can take a mile or more for a big freight train to haul itself down to a complete stop. In addition, it takes more than just intuition for a locomotive engineer to discern when and where he can take his train into a particular track. That is why, from the earliest days, railroads have tried to come up with lineside signals to control rail traffic efficiently and, above all, safely.

In the early days of railroading, such things were not all that easy to do. Some of the earliest lineside signals were a little strange by today's standards. In one early method, a station agent would haul up a series of colored balls on a rope to tell the engineer whether or not he had the right of way. Woe to the locomotive driver who ignored a black ball signal! (That's where we get the expression to *blackball* someone; that is, to forbid him to proceed.) Another odd type of signal was the smash board, used on rail bridges into the 1930s. The name was quite literal; if the bridge was open for river traffic and the train ran the usual signal, a large board with a "STOP" message would be stretched across the track—and the engineer would smash right through it

if he ignored it. The noise of the splintering board would be sure to get his attention!

These odd signals soon gave way to the more conventional signal devices we know today: dwarf signals for switch yards, block signals, semaphores, and so on. In prewar years Lionel even issued a huge position signal with many lights, the 440 Signal Bridge for Standard gauge, but in the postwar era only Marx tried such a signal. Lionel concentrated heavily upon the most familiar light signals, such as the 151 Semaphore and the big, handsome 153 twin-light Block Signal. Since Lionel operators wanted to imitate what they saw around them, excellent sales resulted.

The modern era saw production of the same kinds of trackside signal devices right from the start. The plentiful 163 Block Target Signal, last marketed by Lionel in the postwar era in a plain white box, was one of the first signal devices to emerge. The 2163, as it was renumbered, came as a postwar leftover in the Type I "Banner" box, and sometimes it even came with the two-light signal head instead of the single target. (These signal heads would fit on the same bracket.) However, the big metal 151 Semaphore and 153 Block Signal would not return. Instead, Fundimensions completely redesigned the semaphore into a plastic unit that worked very well, even if the motion was the reverse of the old 151. Fundimensions then concentrated on the postwar 353 for its two-light block signal model instead of the 153.

Lionel Trains Inc. brought back the popular two-track signal bridge, complete with the interchangeable signal heads of the old 450. The single signal bridge also returned, which was good for operators because the postwar version had become scarce. Even the old 161 Mail Pickup Set returned to the pages of the modern-era catalogs.

Like many other modern-era accessories, the 2115 Dwarf Signal (right) and 2282 Illuminated Bumper (left) were based on postwar predecessors.

If you use insulated rail sections to operate the lineside signals, they will operate in a prototypical fashion. For example, if you have a 2163 Block Target Signal with red and green lights, use two insulated tracks. Locate one on the other side of your layout from the signal and run the wire that illuminates the green bulb to the insulated rail. Then locate the other insulated section at the signal; hook up the ground wire to the center rail and the wire controlling the red lamp to the insulated rail. If you've judged your distances correctly, the green lamp will go on when your train reaches the far rail. As the train continues, it will trigger the red lamp just about the time the last car leaves the rail activating the green signal. That will go out, and when the train passes the signal, the red lamp will go out as well. You can't do that with a pressure contactor!

Lionel's trackside signals have always been a lot of fun to watch. The semaphores add motion to a layout as well as light; all of them create just the right aura of realism and control that operators desire. They are a rightful part of Lionel's miniature world, and it is good that both Fundimensions and LTI have continued that proud heritage.

2115 DWARF SIGNAL, 1984–87

Gray body, black twin-light lens hood; uses pin-type bulbs; Type III box. This accessory was always a popular little item on Lionel layouts featuring ladder tracks and complex switch yards, which is where real railroads used these lights. The Fundimensions version, however, worked more conventionally than did the postwar 148, which used a special manually operated slide switch similar in appearance to the 364C On-Off Switch. All modern-era versions operate just like the other lineside signals: by pressure contactor or

	Exc	Mint

insulated track section. **Cross-references:** PW 148; ME 12704, 12883.

	20	25

2117 BLOCK TARGET SIGNAL, 1985–87

Black base, gray pole, red ladder, black two-light lens hood. This two-lens block signal was similar in appearance and operation to the postwar 353. Although the previously released 2163 was supposed to be a single-lens model, it often came with a two-lens hood because both hoods would fit and Fundimensions was trying to use up its inventory of spare parts. **Cross-references:** PW 253, 353; ME 2163, 12832.

	20	25

2151 SEMAPHORE, 1978–83

Light brown plastic base, black pole, yellow- and black-striped semaphore arm, red ladder, red and green jewel lights; raises as train approaches. Rather than revive the popular postwar 151, Fundimensions decided to redesign the semaphore completely. The result was a plastic model that was more fragile than its predecessor, but also lacked the troublesome toothed gear operation. In the case of the 151, the semaphore blade lowered when the signal turned red. However, in the 2151 the normal green position of the blade was horizontal, and the blade was raised so that the red lens showed when the accessory was operated. This is incorrect prototypically, but it is doubtful that this has been a major element in considering the item for purchase. Generally speaking, the 2151 is more reliable in operation than the 151. **Cross-reference:** ME 12727.

	20	25

The 2163 Auto Block Target Signal was the first signal device made by Fundimensions. Note how similar the final postwar version (left) is to Version B with its medium tan base (center). Version C features a dark tan base (right).

Exc Mint

2163 AUTO BLOCK TARGET SIGNAL, 1970–78

Green light switches to red as train approaches; 7½" high, contactor, L-19R red bulb, L-19G green bulb, both with pins. Some Type I boxes claim height of 9", but this is incorrect and Type II and III boxes correct the error. This was the first of the signal devices produced by Fundimensions; as a result, some early examples show extremely interesting packaging and may come in leftover plain white boxes with black printing on only one end; reader comments concerning this are requested. This accessory was known to come in plain white boxes in the last year of postwar production. Early examples came with a single target lens, as in postwar production, but 1972 and later examples often had a two-lens head (they are interchangeable). In the listings below, note that three distinct shades of the tan base are found. We would like clarification as to which of these shades were more likely postwar leftovers and which were Fundimensions production, whatever the stamping on the underside of the base. **Cross-references:** PW 253, 353; ME 2117, 12832.

(A) Light tan base, Type I or Type II box.

20 25

(B) Medium tan base, Type II box.

20 25

(C) Dark tan base, brass-colored wire thumbscrews instead of nickel. Box type not known, may be plain white box as in late postwar era or Type I box. Fundimensions used plain white boxes for rolling stock in these years, so that type is a possibility.

20 25

(D) Same as (B), but leftover postwar 163 repackaged in Type I box labeled "Automatic Single Block Signal." (Type II boxes were labeled "Automatic Block Target Signal".) Unusual piece and packaging.

NRS

2311 MECHANICAL SEMAPHORE KIT, 1982–92

Black base and trip lever, white pole and semaphore arm, black stripes, red and green simulated lights on arm. A later version of the 2312 made in kit form for inclusion in many sets as well as separate sale. Unlike the 2312, it is not illuminated. **Cross-reference:** ME 2312.

4 8

Lionel Trains Inc. offered signal bridges for double-track main lines (the 12724 on the left) and single-track lines (the 12763 on the right).

	Exc	Mint

2312 MECHANICAL SEMAPHORE, 1973–77

Identical in construction to the 2311, but it came ready-made, and two copper track contacts in the base illuminated the signal. **Cross-reference:** ME 2311.

	5	10

12704 DWARF SIGNAL, 1988–93

Maroon signal body, black lens hood, red and green pin-base lights. This LTI reissue of the dwarf signal follows the pattern of the early LTI accessories: the substitution of brighter colors. It operates like the 2115, with a pressure contactor or insulated track section. **Cross-references:** PW 148; ME 2115, 12883.

	20	25

12724 TWO-TRACK SIGNAL BRIDGE, 1988–90

Black metal girder structure, light gray plastic bases, two black plastic two-light lens hoods. This large accessory is a nearly direct remake of the desirable

postwar 450. Like its predecessor, it features two signal heads that can be installed to face in the same or different directions, depending upon how the trains are run. Louis Marx & Co. and some smaller firms offered similar structures. A method for making this and other block signals operate in a more prototypical fashion is described in the introduction to this chapter. **Cross-references:** PW 450; ME 12895.

	45	60

12727 OPERATING SEMAPHORE, 1989–97

Dark maroon base, black pole, yellow arm with black stripes. Yet another LTI reissue of a Fundimensions accessory in brighter colors. It operates in the same way the 2151 does. **Cross-reference:** ME 2151.

		CP

12729 MAIL PICKUP SET, 1988–91 and 1995

Black base, red pole, semaphore arm and swinging arm, large red magnetic mailbag. The postwar 161 is dif-

More popular postwar accessories were revived by LTI, starting in 1988 with the 12729 Mail Pickup Set (left). The 12727 Operating Semaphore (center) followed the next year, and the 12760 Automatic Highway Flasher (right) was brought out in 1990.

Exc Mint

ficult to find intact, so operators welcomed the reissue of the accessory. It is questionable how many of these reissued sets have actually been used, however, because the operation of the accessory depends upon gluing a magnet to the side of a car, and not many collectors would deface a car in that way. The pole holds a large mailbag; when the button is pressed, the arm swings towards the track so the magnet on the car can swipe the bag off the arm as the car goes by. In the 1950s, The A. C. Gilbert Co. included in its American Flyer line a baggage car with a mail hook that worked much better; the hook mechanism was inside the car, and it extended from the car to swipe the bag off a stationary pole. The success of the Lionel accessory's operation depends upon exact placement of the pole and its mechanism. **Cross-reference:** PW 161.

15   20

12763 SINGLE SIGNAL BRIDGE, 1990–91 and 1993

Gray plastic base, black girder structure, black twin-lens lamp hood, red and green pin-base bulbs. This nearly direct remake of the postwar model enabled more operators to use this accessory, since the 452 is scarce. The signal hangs over the track and is secured by a metal rod extending from the base; the rod has a screw hole to allow fastening to the platform. **Cross-references:** PW 452; ME 12894.

30   35

12832 BLOCK TARGET SIGNAL, 1993–97

Tuscan plastic base, light cap and two-lens lamp hood, black metal ladder, gray pole. This LTI model is a

Exc Mint

direct remake of the earlier 2117 with two-lens hood, except for different colors. Like its contemporaries, it comes in a Type VI box. **Cross-references:** PW 252, 353; ME 2117, 2163.

25   35

12883 DWARF SIGNAL, 1995–97

Black base, Tuscan two-lens hood, red and green pin-base bulbs. Identical to 12704, except for different color of lens hood. **Cross-references:** PW 148; ME 2115, 12704.

CP

12894 SINGLE SIGNAL BRIDGE, 1995–97

Black plastic base, gray-painted metal girder structure, black ladder, black two-lens lamp hood, red and green pin-base bulbs. Identical to LTI's 12724, except for color; see that entry for comments on operation. **Cross-references:** PW 452; ME 12724.

CP

12895 TWO-TRACK SIGNAL BRIDGE, 1995–97

Gray plastic bases, Tuscan-painted metal girder structure, Tuscan ladders, two black two-lens lamp hoods, red and green pin-base bulbs. Identical to LTI's 12724, except for different colors; see that entry for comments on operation. **Cross-references:** PW 450; ME 12724.

CP

6

BRIDGES, TRESTLES, AND TUNNELS

It so happens that the work which is likely to be our most durable monument, and to convey some knowledge of us to the most remote posterity, is a work of bare utility; not a shrine, not a fortress, not a palace, but a bridge.
— Montgomery Schuyler, *Harper's Weekly*, 1883

INTRODUCTION

In his excellent PBS documentary about the Brooklyn Bridge, Ken Burns (among others) made the point that a bridge is a very special piece of architecture. Because it transcends obstacles and reaches to the sky like a gigantic work of art, a bridge can be symbolic of humanity's hopes for its future. A bridge can also be a statement of optimism that people have come to a particular place to stay for good and to trust in progress. Burns was talking about one unique bridge, of course, but he might have been talking about many other great bridges: Verrazano-Narrows, the Firth of Forth, the Golden Gate, or New York's Hell Gate Bridge. That's where Lionel comes into the story.

In the prewar era, Lionel produced one of the most magnificent accessories of its history, the 300 Hell Gate Bridge, originals of which are highly prized. This huge bridge was Joshua Lionel Cowen's statement of confidence in the future when it was first made in 1928; except for scale length it closely resembled its prototype, and it was made in a beautiful green and cream color scheme (later red and ivory). Even during the Great Depression, Lionel continued to produce the Hell Gate Bridge, right up to the end of prewar production in 1942.

Lionel's postwar bridge offerings were not quite that ambitious, but there was always the great 313

Bascule Bridge, which was not only massive but also operational. A large 213 Lift Bridge was planned for the company's fiftieth anniversary in 1950, but it never got beyond the prototype stage. Fundimensions continued the production of many fine bridges, but it took Richard Kughn's tenure to produce the huge operational 12782 Operating Lift Bridge, the largest Lionel accessory of all time. We could look upon the production of this bridge symbolically as a statement of confidence in Lionel's future by Lionel Trains Inc., just as the Hell Gate Bridge had been for the original Lionel Corporation sixty-three years previously.

There are heroic stories associated with tunnels, too; one thinks of the unbelievable feat of the Simplon Pass Tunnel drilled through the Alps into solid rock. However, the presence of ready-made Styrofoam tunnels in the modern market has prevented Fundimensions and LTI from producing more than the portals for the tunnels—with one noteworthy exception (see 2714 entry).

Trestles, however, are quite another story. The 110 and 111 Graduated and Elevated Trestle Sets were a fixture throughout much of the postwar period and in all the years of the modern era. This is fitting, since trestle bridges of all types have been a part of American railroading since its beginning. Because some trestles in the early years were rather flimsy, opportunities for great heroism were plentiful; one thinks of the Kate Shelley story in Iowa, where a young girl of fifteen saved a train from a wreck on a washed-out trestle on a wild and stormy night in the summer of 1881. Lionel's trestles, however, were sturdy and well-designed when they were properly assembled. The plastic clips of the modern-era trestles seem to hold the track in place just as well as the metal plates and screws of the postwar examples.

Being able to raise the track and watch a train run high over the tabletop has always provided opera-
tors with pleasure. To ensure that this thrill would be available, Fundimensions began cataloging the
2110 Graduated Trestle Set (right) and the 2111 Elevated Trestle Set (left).

The next time you assemble a trestle set, place a tunnel atop your track (old or new), or span gaps with a plate girder or extension bridge, remember that such structures symbolize, in their miniature way, the confidence and faith you have in your own little empire. With their incorporation, it is as if you have said to yourself, "I too have come to stay."

2110 GRADUATED TRESTLE SET, 1970–88

Twenty-two trestle pieces graduated from 3/16" to 4 3/4" high, most came with plastic clips, although a few early Fundimensions pieces in Type I boxes included leftover postwar metal clips, plates and screws. This set is designed to raise the track from platform level to a height of 4 3/4" in a space of 5 feet. Since that is a fairly steep rise (necessarily so), trains without Magnetraction are somewhat limited in the load they

can carry. If an operator is worried about the variation in speed up or down, there is a fairly easy procedure to ease the problem. Purchase two small transformers; even the common postwar 25-watt ones should do. Insulate both the upgrade and the downgrade of the trestle set from the platform-level section of the layout. (Insulating pins in the center rails will do this.) Wire one of the small transformers to the upgrade and the other to the downgrade. Then adjust the operating voltage of the small transformers so that the locomotive receives more power on the upgrade and less on the downgrade. The plastic clips for the trestles were changed in 1988 so the clips could also be used with O gauge track. However, most serious postwar train operators prefer the old metal clips and plates, which are still readily available. Many used sets are missing the lowest trestle bent because it is just a simple 3/8" plate. The bents are labeled so that "A" is the tallest and "K" the smallest. Modern-era versions have been made in

Exc   Mint

gray, brown, and black. **Cross-references:** PW 110; ME 12754.

(A) Dark brown trestles, Type I box; leftover postwar pieces and sometimes metal clips. Came with postwar instruction sheet.

15   20

(B) Light gray trestles, Type II or III packaging, black plastic clips.

10   15

2111 ELEVATED TRESTLE SET, 1970–88

Ten 4¾"-high piers identical to tall piers in 2110. This set is used to expand the Graduated Trestle Set. Like the 2110, it came in brown, gray, or black; the packaging follows the same pattern. **Cross-references:** PW 111; ME 12755.

(A) Dark brown trestles, leftover postwar pieces, Type I packaging. Earliest production came with leftover metal clips, plates, screws, and postwar instruction sheet.

15   20

(B) Light gray trestles, Type II or III packaging, black plastic clips.

10   15

2113 TUNNEL PORTALS, 1984–87

Gray plastic stonework, "LIONEL" and circle-L logo molded into portal. The Fundimensions reissue of the postwar tunnel portals has become difficult to find. These portals are a darker shade of gray than their postwar counterparts, and instead of "1957" and "Hillside" they have "LIONEL" molded into them. The portals were sold in sets of two and came in a Type III box, unlike the LTI issue, which comes in a cello bag. **Cross-references:** PW 920-2; ME 12896.

20   30

2122 EXTENSION BRIDGE, 1976–87

Two gray plastic piers, brown plastic girder structure, black metal bridge base, requires assembly; 24" long, 5" wide, piers 7" high, overall height with piers is 11¾". This long-running Fundimensions accessory is similar but not identical to the postwar 315. Unlike later issues, it has an arched top. The large bridge comes with two gray rock piers, which were later sold separately. Unlike later issues, this bridge is not illuminated. **Cross-references:** PW 315; ME 12721.

(A) Brown sides and top.

30   40

(B) Same as (A), but mismatched maroon plastic top; unusual variation.

30   40

2214 GIRDER BRIDGE, 1970–87

Black or brownish-black anodized metal base, dark or light gray plastic side girders embossed "LIONEL", comes knocked down or assembled. For knocked down versions, plastic sides must be screwed on with eight Phillips-head screws; 10" long and 4½" wide. This long-running, familiar little bridge has been in the Lionel catalog without interruption since its introduction in 1953,

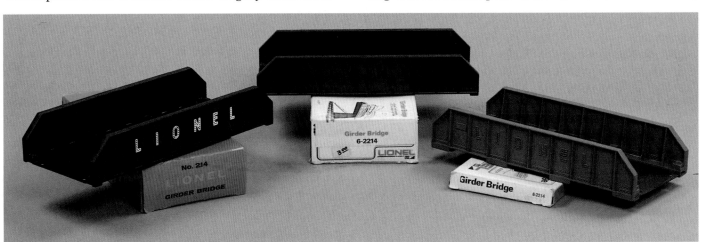

The sturdy little girder bridge has been a fixture in the Lionel line since 1940. During the modern era, the 2214 carried on the tradition identified with the 214 (left). The 2214 was available with dark gray plastic sides (center) or light gray sides (right).

A brand-new accessory with great operating potential was the 2317 Operating Drawbridge, which Fundimensions cataloged from 1975 through 1981.

and its 314 predecessor goes back to 1940. Obviously, it is a very popular accessory, and that has led to some interesting variations in its product development sequence in the modern era. It is possible that the first versions of the 2214 came as postwar 214 leftovers in a plain white box, but confirmation of this is lacking. It is known for certain that postwar leftovers were marketed fully assembled in Type I boxes. When Fundimensions produced its own version of the bridge, the accessory came knocked down and the girder structure was changed from screw assembly to slot-and-groove assembly; the girders simply snapped into the sides of the metal base (which still retained the screw holes). This version also came in a smaller Type I box. For some reason, this version was abandoned in early 1972 and the accessory reverted to screw-on assembly, coming in Type II and III boxes for the rest of its Fundimensions run. Possibly the slot-and-groove assembly came loose because of vibrations from the passing trains. The earliest versions are difficult to find. **Cross-references:** PW 214, ME 12730.

	Exc	Mint

(A) 1970–early 1971, flat black girder sides, white-outlined Lionel lettering, black-anodized base with postwar markings, comes assembled in larger Type I box. This is a leftover 214 with postwar markings repackaged into a Type I Fundimensions box.

15   25

(B) 1971–early 1972, smaller Type I box, knocked down assembly, dark gray plastic sides, outlined "LIONEL" with MPC logo to left, black-anodized metal base faintly embossed "No. 2214 BRIDGE BY LIONEL MPC Mt. CLEMENS, MICH. MADE IN U.S.A." Method of attaching base differs from later versions; girders fit into base by means of slots molded into girder sides and have no screws for assembly, snap-together.

15   25

(C) early 1973, light gray girders, comes assembled in unusual Stone Container Corp. box similar to that found on examples of 2256 Station Platform. Dated

The 2714 Tunnel, cataloged from 1975 to 1977, had no marks identifying it as a Lionel product. Collectors needed to rely on its colorful box to know who made it.

Exc   Mint

as early 1973 based upon that example; very unusual packaging.

15   25

(D) 1973–87, Type II or (later) Type III box, light gray girders. Earliest production pieces retain MPC logo; later ones omit it. Screws provided for assembly; girders revert to postwar construction.

8   10

2317 OPERATING DRAWBRIDGE, 1975–81

Tan base, dark brown plastic piers, dark gray span, gray supports, five pressure binding posts on right side of base, olive green tender house with light brown roof, dark brown door and steps, with one full length of O27 track and two half sections. Very complex to wire, but excellent operating action. Difficult to find mint with original box and wire and plastic binding strips for packaging intact and in place. This was Fundimensions' first original operating accessory, even if the operating design and wiring came from the postwar 313 Bascule Bridge. Its appearance is contemporary, and its attractive design and colors made it popular with operators. Note that it was designed to work with the O27 track prevalent at the time, but it can be modified to work with O gauge track. When the button is pushed, a bell rings and the lift part of the bridge raises, cutting off power to the train on the

The 2716 Short Extension Bridge was actually a snap-together kit that added interest to large and small model railroads alike. This photograph was originally used in the 1991 catalog.

Exc   Mint

upper part of the bridge and allowing another train to pass through the bridge gap beneath. A second push of the button lowers the lift part of the bridge and restores power to the upper train, stopping any train on the lower track. The 2317 can be wired for fully automatic operation.

120   150

2714 TUNNEL, 1975–77

White Styrofoam tunnel in two longitudinal snap-together sections painted various shades of brown and green for scenic effect, 15½" x 13½" x 10". The tunnel was packed in a very large Type II box; extremely hard to find in original box, which is virtually the only way the tunnel can be identified as a Lionel product! This relatively short straight-track tunnel is probably one of the most difficult to find of all Lionel accessories of any era because it must be packaged in its original box to identify the accessory as Lionel issue. The tunnel itself carries no Lionel markings whatsoever and is virtually indistinguishable from the many Styrofoam equivalents sold in toy and train stores during the holiday season. This was a strange marketing effort by Fundimensions because this tunnel sold at a price disadvantage. Most operators and collectors have never even seen one of these tunnels in its original box. The fragility of the tunnel and the large size of the box mean that few of these tunnels have survived in their original packaging. Both

Exc   Mint

Excellent and Mint values require original box to establish both identity and values cited.

40   50

2716 SHORT EXTENSION BRIDGE, 1987–95

Measures 10" x 6½" x 4½"; brown plastic girder structures in plastic kit form, no metal base, girders are black instead of brown. When LTI ran an accessory from the Fundimensions era, it usually chose a five-digit number. In a few cases the original Fundimensions number was retained and given a "6" prefix for cataloging. This, however, is the only known case where a carryover successor was assigned a new four-digit number instead of the usual five-digit one. The brown girder structure of the Fundimensions accessory was changed to black, but otherwise this bridge is the same as the 2717. It came as a kit packed in a Type III box or as an inclusion in many starter train sets. In 1993–95, it has also come packed in a cello bag instead of a box. **Cross-reference: ME 2717.**
CP

2717 SHORT EXTENSION BRIDGE, 1977–86 and 1989–91

Measures 10" x 6½" x 4½"; brown plastic girder structures in plastic kit form, no metal base. This

Layout builders have enjoyed working with the 12770 Arch-Under Bridge ever since Lionel Trains revived this postwar accessory in 1990.

	Exc	Mint

long-running Fundimensions bridge was sold separately in a Type III box and included in many inexpensive train sets. Its girders are the same color as the much bigger 2214, and its overall appearance is similar. Several of these bridges can be combined to make up one long truss bridge.

5   **7**

12721 ILLUMINATED EXTENSION BRIDGE WITH ROCK PIERS, 1989

Medium brown bridge structure, gray rock piers, arched top segment with red light at top, stamped steel base. Similar to 2122, except for added light and piers; contrasts with 12772. This accessory, produced for just one year, has become somewhat hard to find because its structure was modified for 1990 and its catalog number changed. It is really a modified Fundimensions 2122 with an added blinking light and newly designed rock piers. **Cross-references:** PW 315; ME 2122, 12772.

40   **50**

12730 PLATE GIRDER BRIDGE, 1988–97

Black plastic girders, white-outlined "LIONEL" lettering, chemically blackened metal base, sold knocked down to be assembled by purchaser. With its black girders and white outlined "LIONEL" lettering, this LTI reissue of the 2214 looks most like its postwar 214

predecessor. Sold in Type VI box; in recent years the accessory has come packaged in a cello bag. Cross-**references:** PW 214; ME 2214.

CP

12744 ROCK PIERS, 1989–92 and 1994–97

Two large plastic 4¾"-high simulated rock piles that support bridges as part of elevated trestle layouts. They are identical to those supplied with the 12721 and 12772 extension bridges. They came in a Type VI box earlier, but since 1994 have been sold in a cello bag. The catalog description for the 12772 Extension Bridge states these piers have been modified so several bridges can be connected together. Probably the base was modified so that the edges of the piers would abut properly for multiple-bridge installation.

CP

12754 GRADUATED TRESTLE SET, 1989–97

Twenty-two graduated trestle pieces in dark brown; height ranges from ⅜" to 4¾". The usual set of twenty-two graduated trestle pieces follows the pattern of its predecessors, but the plastic clips included with the set have been modified to work with O gauge track as well as O27. Packaged in Type VI box. **Cross-references:** PW 110; ME 2110.

CP

The 12782 Operating Lift Bridge ranks as one of the most spectacular of all Lionel accessories, regardless of era. It brought to fruition a design originally illustrated in the 1950 catalog but never mass-produced. This series of photographs from the 1991 catalog shows the span being raised.

	Exc	Mint

12755 ELEVATED TRESTLE SET, 1989–97

Ten dark brown 4¾"-high pieces to extend 12754 set. **Cross-references:** PW 111; ME 2111.

CP

	Exc	Mint

12770 ARCH-UNDER BRIDGE, 1990–97

Light gray plastic snap-together girders and support feet, black stamped steel deck. This LTI remake of the scarce postwar 332 has sold very well during its

Exc Mint

production time. The catalog lists the height of the bridge as 4⅞", but this cannot be correct for it to match the highest piers of the trestle sets, which are 4¾". This bridge's deck appearance shows trains off to their maximum advantage because there is no intervening girder structure. **Cross-reference:** PW 332.

CP

12772 ILLUMINATED EXTENSION BRIDGE WITH ROCK PIERS, 1990–97

Dark gray bridge structure with flat top segment (as opposed to arch of 2122 and 12721), stamped-steel base, gray rock piers, red light atop bridge structure. After just one year of LTI production, the 12721 was modified to create this model, which presents an entirely different, more massive appearance. Like the 12721, it includes the new rock piers and the blinking light atop the bridge. Instead of the arched girder structure of the 12721, this model has a level top structure and larger criss-cross support girders. **Cross-references:** PW 321; ME 2122, 12721.

CP

12782 OPERATING LIFT BRIDGE, 1991–92

Light gray structure, black ladders and catwalk detail, extremely large (29½" x 8" x 19¼"!) operating span corresponding to 213 announced in 1950 but never made. When Lionel operators and collectors got their first look at this stupendous accessory, their general reaction was "Wow!" No wonder: this operating bridge is the largest accessory ever made by Lionel. How large? Its packing case will not fit in most car trunks! It is so large that it needs its own power supply to operate properly. The operator is supplied with a rectangular control box that has controls to raise or lower the moving bridge surface, blast the warning horn, and ring the warning bell. The horn is loud enough to notify most of a city block that the bridge is operating. A single motor operates a series of gears and pulley strings taking the bridge up and changing

Exc Mint

the signal lights for the tracks to red and the ones for the "river traffic" to green. The warning bell (if selected) is continuous, and the horn blows by operator selection. Yellow-green strobe lights rotate atop the bridge piers while the power is on. The upright spans for the bridge are also illuminated. As counterweights keep the center span raised, power to the track is cut off while the span is being lifted and restored when it touches its base again. Seldom, if ever, has a more spectacular operating accessory been marketed by *any* maker of toy trains. The impracticality of this accessory for most layouts has not stopped it from being in demand by operators and collectors alike.

450   600

12896 TUNNEL PORTALS, 1995–97

Dark gray unpainted plastic with "LIONEL" and circle-L logo molded into portal atop entrance arch. These LTI portals appear to be identical to the Fundimensions portals except for their being a darker gray. Instead of a box, they are sold in pairs in a large cello bag. **Cross-references:** PW 920-2; ME 2113.

CP

12948 OPERATING BASCULE BRIDGE, 1997

Catalog shows postwar colors: green base for both track section and shack (which will probably be unpainted), yellow shack with red roof and window inserts, silver-painted bridge structure. This fabled postwar accessory's reissue is eagerly awaited by collectors and operators alike; at the time of this writing it had not been issued. The catalog copy states that the bridge will be all metal, just like its postwar counterpart. However, the spring-motor drive of the postwar version has been replaced by the ubiquitous can-motor drive system, which has been quite reliable for Lionel in its applications and provides a smooth operation. The catalog shows the accessory in its postwar configuration. **Cross-references:** PW 313.

CP

7

BUILDINGS AND SCENERY

A locomotive whistle was a matter of some importance to a railroad engineer. It was tuned and worked, even played, according to his own particular choosing. The whistle was part of the make-up of the man; he was known for it as much as for the engine he drove. . . . But there was no horseplay about tying down the whistle cord. A locomotive whistle blowing without letup meant one thing on the railroad, and to everyone who lived near the railroad. It meant that there was something very wrong.

—David McCullough, *The Johnstown Flood*

INTRODUCTION

The trouble with classifying Lionel's accessories into more or less coherent groupings is that some accessories defy categorization. What does the harried chronicler of accessories do with a whistle shack? It operates, all right, but it doesn't transfer cargo, it isn't a station, and it's definitely not a roadside signal. How about the newsstand? That little accessory certainly has action, but where do you categorize it? One thing this rather eclectic group does have in common: The buildings all add a great deal to the appearance of a layout as a desirable "miniature world." So, let's toss them into the *scenery* chapter on that basis!

As a consequence of this admittedly arbitrary decision, you'll find billboard listings next to diesel horn sheds, flagpoles next to diners, and now even an operating windmill next to the fabulous steam clean and wheel grinding shop! Yes, this is a somewhat arbitrary decision, but the more you think about a layout as a world in miniature, the more it makes sense. As a result, some of the most interesting of all modern-era accessories will be found in this chapter. Some of them

have truly interesting stories to tell, such as the 2125 Whistle Shack, surely one of the greatest accessory curios in Lionel's history. Here's a gem about the revival of the Animated Newsstand, the Fundimensions 2308: Note that the little terrier is still running around the fire hydrant as he did in the original postwar 128. How many collectors and operators know that the designer of this accessory, Frank Pettit, modeled that dog after his son's terrier, Chris? Even in the earliest Fundimensions billboard sets, the Myco Foam Packaging billboard relates an interesting attempt by General Mills to use the foam padding in sets as potential houses and buildings for layouts!

It is clear, therefore, that this group of accessories has more than its share of Lionel lore and legend. Who would have thought, back in the highly competitive 1950s, that Lionel would one day produce a billboard set with a sign advertising its one-time chief rival, American Flyer? Could anyone in postwar times have foreseen the Animated Newsstand being turned into the wacky yet charming Animated Refreshment Stand with its huge rotating ice cream cone? Read on, Lionel aficionados. The adventure of this chapter now begins!

2125 WHISTLING FREIGHT SHED, 1971

White shed body, bright red door, window inserts, and toolshed lid, green roof (slight variations of the green shade exist), dark brown base, postwar-type motor. Type I box; mint condition requires presence of box, which is fragile. Came with leftover no. 90 Controller. Very hard to find, especially with original Type I box.

The tale of this whistle shed represents one of the most interesting stories concerning the transitional

Left: The 2125 Whistling Freight Shed was cataloged in 1971 only. It used a leftover postwar motor, and the light was illuminated only when the whistle was activated. Right: The 2126 Whistling Freight Shed was cataloged from 1976 through 1978 and was not equipped with a light. The green door with twelve small windows indicates this is Version B.

period between the postwar and the Fundimensions years. This accessory resembles its predecessor a great deal, as well it should. The white housing structure is a leftover part and, most important, so is the large AC motor with its impeller casing. To be efficient, Fundimensions decided (in this and several other cases) to use up any leftover parts on hand. Either because the roofs and bases were not as plentiful as the housings and motors or because the firm wanted to give the whistle shack a new look, the old molds were used to turn out bases and roofs in different colors from the old model. One other element of this accessory was different: It was illuminated. Apparently there was a relatively late decision to put a light in the shack, and the easiest way to do that was to put Fahnestock clips on both ends of the metal rods securing the bases to the housings instead of just at the top. A 12-volt automotive-type lamp (the same one Chrysler used for its side marker lights for many years) was placed in a plastic socket and attached to the upper clips.

The instruction sheet told purchasers to wire the accessory from the bottom clips, unlike the postwar instructions, which told them to bring the wires up through the house to the top clips. Of course the only way the lamp could light would be when the button was pushed to make the whistle blow! That's a very strange effect, and the Fundimensions instruction sheet makes it clear that the accessory was meant to operate that way. It would have been more effective to provide a third rod and clip set on the housing, as was done with the 2145 Automatic Gateman, but perhaps the rush to get the accessory to market precluded that.

What remains is a fascinating little accessory that was discontinued after just one year, probably because the supply of postwar motor-impeller units ran out. It is highly doubtful that more than 1,000 of these little shacks exist today, making this accessory scarcer than any regular-production postwar accessory, even the 397 Operating Diesel-Type Coal Loader with a yellow

	Exc	Mint

generator and yard light. It's easy to chuckle at the strange action of this whistle shack, but the ingenuity of Fundimensions in getting it out is undeniable.

As with the 125s, the heavy AC motor and whistle casing is held to the bottom of the housing structure by double-stick tape. Over time, this tape loses its adhesive ability and the motor falls from the bottom of the house. To remedy this, acquire new strips of double-sided foam tape (3M markets it for picture hanging) and scrape the remnants of old tape from the shed base and the whistle casing. Apply the new tape to the top of the casing and press back into place. Your 2125 (or 125, for that matter) is good for many more years! **Cross-references:** PW 125; ME 2126.

(A) Green roof, as described above.

	60	75

(B) Same as (A), but extra wiring posts added to base to control whistle motor; main clips activate light only. Appears to be a Service Station postfactory alteration. Reader confirmation would be welcomed.

	60	75

(C) Same as (A), but maroon roof, same as postwar model. Authenticated from original box; probable use of leftover roof.

	60	75

2126 WHISTLING FREIGHT SHED, 1976–87

Dark brown plastic base, light yellow shed, green door and windows, opaque window in nonopening door, green toolshed lid, lighter brown plastic roof, diode-activated whistle motor. Found with two types of doors: one has two large windows (1976–77); the other has twelve smaller windows (1978–87). Curiously, it was quite some time before Fundimensions got around to marketing a replacement for the short-lived 2125. When it finally produced the 2126, the whistle mechanism was different. It still featured a fan impeller to drive air through a tuned plastic whistle chamber, but now the motor was a DC can-type motor with an AC rectifier. This whistle worked very well, but its whistle sound was anemic compared to the powerful AC motor of its predecessor. That didn't stop it from enjoying a long catalog life. **Cross-references:** PW 125; ME 2125.

(A) Brown plastic roof.

	30	40

(B) Same as (A), but green plastic roof (possibly leftover from 2125 production).

	30	40

	Exc	Mint

2127 DIESEL HORN SHED, 1976–87

Measures 4⅞" high, 6" x 6" light tan plastic base, red building, white toolshed lid, white door, frosted window, gray roof. Same door variation as 2126. In appearance, the 2127 followed the pattern set by the 2125 and 2126; beyond that this accessory was a new Fundimensions design. It was powered by a 9-volt battery inserted into a clip in the base. This battery was connected to an electronic chipboard, which connected to a small speaker at the base of a cardboard tube. The speaker sounded the diesel horn (rather nasally) and the cardboard tube acted like a ducted port in a stereo system speaker to amplify the sound. The only trouble with the Diesel Horn Shed was that when the battery wore down, some awfully strange and strained sounds would come out of that speaker! Many operators do not realize that the tone of the horn can be adjusted. There is a small circular piece of plastic with a little slot on the circuit board. If the slot is turned very slightly with a small screwdriver, the tone of the horn can be made higher or lower. However, the horn is sensitive to the slightest motion of this slot and its tone is difficult to adjust at best. The 2127 is fairly obsolete as an operating accessory because its LTI successor sounds a great deal more realistic. This version is unique because it requires no connection to the transformer of any kind.

	30	40

2180 ROAD SIGN SET, 1977–97

Set of sixteen white plastic highway and railroad signs with black lettering. They are designed much like their predecessors, but are in one piece rather than the plastic pole and metal base of the postwar sets. **Cross-reference:** PW 309.

		CP

2181 TELEPHONE POLES, 1977–97

Set of ten light brown one-piece plastic poles, each 7" high. This set of telephone poles resembles those put out by Bachmann for Plasticville much more than they do the massive ones put out by Lionel in the early postwar years. The poles in the postwar set were equipped with separate metal bases that attached to the track; their modern-era counterparts are cast in one piece. **Cross-reference:** PW 150.

		CP

2308 ANIMATED NEWSSTAND, 1982–83

Dark green stand (considerably darker than postwar version), white "LIONEL NEWS" lettering, row of

Here is a small yet representative sample of the colorful billboards that were included with the 2710 and 12707 Billboards With Frames offered by Fundimensions and Lionel Trains Inc. between 1970 and 1995.

	Exc	**Mint**

magazines below counter, red roof, small lamp on news counter illuminates when accessory is operated, light tan base, white dog circles red fire hydrant, gray newsboy with painted face and hands, newspaper fits into slot in his hand, painted newsstand operator inside stand, two large thumb nuts on back of base for electrical connections. This Fundimensions reissue of the clever postwar vibrator-operated accessory has become increasingly difficult to find. Aside from the brighter, deeper colors and some updating of the decorative magazines displayed at the stand, this model looks much like its predecessor. When the button activates the accessory, the terrier scampers around the fire hydrant, the news dealer comes forward within the stand, and a newsboy turns to hand him a paper (which is often missing). When LTI modified this accessory, the newsstand was converted into a refreshment stand with a new belt-driven mechanism powered by a DC can motor instead of a vibrator mechanism. The 2308 often jams, especially if it is run at too high a voltage. Be sure the upright spring inside the housing is located within the elongated slot and the mechanism turns freely before operating it again. **Cross-references:** PW 128; ME 12729.

150   **175**

	Exc	**Mint**

2320 FLAG POLE KIT, 1983–87

Fabric American flag, blue Lionel pennant with white lettering, brown plastic base, four sponge corner plots (sponge is less dense than on postwar version), pole is 11" high. Embossed on underside: "PART NO. 00-0089-003 / LIONEL CORPORATION / 1983 CPG." A version of this accessory was made for the Lionel Operating Trains Society in 1984; further description of that version is needed. This Fundimensions reissue of the scarce postwar model has one obvious difference: a 50-star flag instead of the 48-star version of the postwar years. (Alaska and Hawaii did not become states until 1959.) The little sponges that supposedly represent bushes are much more obviously nylon than on the postwar versions. The blue Lionel pennant is retained, but most postwar versions have faded to a bright violet by this time. **Cross-references:** PW 89; ME 12898.

20   **25**

2710 BILLBOARDS WITH FRAMES, 1970–84

Five plastic frames in a box with a strip of five billboards, just like the postwar 310 set. There is an interesting progression of variation in the earliest examples of this accessory. The earliest cardstock billboards have a lavender bordering instead of the dark green used on most postwar examples, but these are still late postwar billboards. The light green frames are Fundimensions products; they have "STANDARD" in an oval on the ribbed bottom. The inside of these frames are stamped "2710 BILL BOARD MT. CLEMENS, MICH. MADE IN U.S.A." and Lionel logo. However, many of the earliest sets in Type I boxes have the dark green leftover postwar frames; some sets have even been seen to have a mix of the two frames. See the list below for changes in the billboards. **Cross-reference:** PW 310.

(A) Type I box dated 8-70, five dark green leftover postwar frames with 310 markings, strip of five public service and other billboards: U.S. Bonds (2), Education (2), and Get A Dodge. (1).

        10   **12**

(B) Same as (A), but billboards differ: Sheraton, MPC, Kenner, Parker Brothers, and Lionel.

        10   **12**

(C) 1970–72, same as (A), but light green frames, MPC logo on inside of frame, Type I box. One example had one dark green postwar and four Fundimensions frames.

        7   **10**

(D) 1973–84, slightly darker green frames, Type II or Type III box, Lionel logo on inside of frame.

        7   **10**

MODERN-ERA BILLBOARD LISTINGS

The following is our third listing of billboards produced by Lionel since 1970. Unless otherwise stated, dates reflect catalog period for a particular billboard. We welcome additions, especially since we suspect there are many uncataloged billboards in existence. In addition, descriptions of the color and lettering schemes are needed with some of the billboards. Examples listed are from G. Halverson, S. Hutchings, R. LaVoie, J. Sawruk, and I. D. Smith Collections.

Note: In 1976, the Train Collectors Association produced six billboards for its bicentennial convention in Philadelphia. While these are desirable from the collector's standpoint, they are not Lionel products. All are white with red and blue printing. They are listed here separately:

TCA 1: 22nd NATIONAL CONVENTION (blue), JUNE 23 to 26, 1976 (red), PHILADELPHIA, PENNSYLVANIA (blue) with red TCA logo and star at left.

TCA 2: 1976 (red, with "9" and "6" in shape of couplers), TRAIN COLLECTORS ASSOCIATION (blue).

TCA 3: Large red eagle, "Hosts To / 22nd Annual Convention / Train Collectors Association Inc." (blue), Delaware Valley Chapter logo in blue at upper left.

TCA 4: 22nd National Convention (blue), TRAIN COLLECTORS ASSOCIATION (red), 1976 coupler logo (red), and TCA shield (blue), SHERATON HOTEL / PHILADELPHIA, PENNSYLVANIA (blue).

TCA 5: Blue rectangular background, locomotive and tender in white, "Train Collectors Association / 22nd National Convention" (red), "Philadelphia / June 23 to 26 / 1976" (blue).

TCA 6: "Hosts To The" (blue) "GREAT EVENT" (large red letters), red star and blue Delaware Valley TCA chapter logo at left.

Fundimensions Production

1. **BUY U. S. SAVINGS BONDS:** 1970–71; stack of $50 bonds wrapped in red, white, and blue flag wrapper on white background.

2. **EDUCATION IS FOR THE BIRDS (The Birds Who Want To Get Ahead):** 1970–71; uncataloged; blue and red lettering on plain white background.

3. **GET A DODGE:** 1970–71; uncataloged; cartoon figure of mule in brown tones, blue lettering on white background.

4. **SHERATON HOTELS:** 1970–71; blue and red rectangles; black lettering and black Sheraton logo.

5. **BETTY CROCKER:** 1970; blue script lettering on white background.

6. **CHEERIOS:** 1970; blue General Mills "G" and red lettering on white background.

7. **LIONEL MPC:** 1970–71; red "LIONEL" in modern typeface; red and blue lettering; red and blue MPC logo on white background.

8. **AUTOLITE:** 1970–71; uncataloged; "Autolite Small Engine Spark Plugs For Work Or Play", red, black, and maroon lettering, green and blue rectangles with lawn mower and motorcycle. Hard to find; came in special version of the 1284 Allegheny set for Ford promotion in 1972.

9. **PLAY-DOH:** 1970–71; uncataloged; "America's Favorite" in blue; child in red pulls can of Play-Doh on red wagon.

10. **FOAM VILLAGE FOR LIONEL BY MYCO:** 1971; uncataloged; conveyor belt carries housing structures out of factory, black "Imagineering for Packaging & Material Handling Systems", yellow background with black conveyor and green building with black "My-T-Veyor" lettering and logo; very hard to find.

11. **LIONEL:** 1972–84; picture of Santa Fe F3 diesel locomotive in red, silver, black, and yellow; "LIONEL" in modern red typeface.

12. **FAMOUS PARKER GAMES:** 1971–76; dark orange background, black lettering and black Parker Brothers "swirl" logo.

13. **CRAFT MASTER:** 1971–84; blue square at left with black and white Craft Master logo and white lettering, light brown portrait of mountain range at right.

14. **MPC MODEL KITS:** 1971–84; dark blue and white MPC logo, red lettering, cars, rocket, and train on yellow and white background.

15. **KENNER TOYS:** 1972–76; yellow and red cartoon bird at right, white lettering on blue background.

16. **SCHLITZ BEER:** 1977–84; beer can and white lettering on red background.

17. **BABY RUTH:** 1977–84; picture of candy bar wrapper, red lettering on white background.

18. **NIBCO WASHERLESS FAUCETS:** 1982; uncataloged; black Nibco logo, red lettering, and picture of faucet on white background. Part of special Nibco Plumbing Products promotion; very difficult to find.

19. **RIDE THE NIBCO EXPRESS:** 1982; uncataloged; black and white lettering and script on dark red background. Part of special Nibco Plumbing Products promotion; very difficult to find.

20. **TAPPAN IS COOKING:** 1982; white lettering on black background, "LIONEL" with red, silver, and yellow Santa Fe set, came with 7908 Tappan boxcar as part of promotional set; difficult to find.

21. **WE'VE / CANNED IT!** (black) / **MOTORCRAFT** (red): 1972; picture of Motorcraft tune-up kit in can packaging with spark plugs, distributor cap, condenser, and points. Part of special Ford Motor Company promotion; very difficult to find.

LIONEL TRAINS INC. PRODUCTION

22A-22B. Double-sided 12707 Billboard. Side A: "Buy U. S. Savings Bonds" in black to left of American flag on white background. Side B: red "Adopt-A-Pet" and white "Support Your Local Humane Society" on blue background with picture of puppy and kitten.

23A-23B. Double-sided billboard with 12707 frames. Side A: large white "BUCKLE UP!" and black "For Safety's Sake" above black seat belt on medium green background. Side B: red "Keep America Beautiful" atop dark, medium, and light blue and gray stylized mountain pass with white background.

24A-24B. Double-sided billboard with 12707 frames. Side A: black "READ . . . AND KNOW THE WORLD!" with multicolored balloon, airplane, Oriental child, locomotive, windmill, etc. on white background. Side B: black "Take The Train" below large red, white, and blue "AMERICAN FLYER LINES" shield logo on white background.

25. **LIONEL VISITOR'S CENTER:** 1994–95; white billboard with red and black crossing signal and gate at upper left and top, black and white steam train at lower left, blue lettering "LIONEL VISITOR'S CENTER / TEN MILES AHEAD / EXIT # 243". Part of 12882 Lighted Billboard accessory.

5031 **TRAIN ACCESSORY KIT/FORD MARKETING CORP., 1972**

Brown corrugated carton with three 2170 street lamps, set of five 2710 billboards: three are regular production (Play-Doh, MPC Model Kits, and Lionel) and two are special (Autolite Small Engine Spark Plugs and Motorcraft: We've Canned It!); 2152 Crossing Gate and a yellow business reply card, "Wholesale Parts Salesmen / . . . WIN AN / ALL AMERICAN / VACATION!". We don't know the full details of this unusual assortment of regular-production Lionel products, but can assume from the contents that some sort of sales competition was involved. We'd like to learn more about this uncataloged promotion; perhaps a Ford salesman could contact us with further information.

NRS

12707 **BILLBOARD SET, 1987–97**

Three large white plastic frames in a new design supplied with three double-sided billboards. Frames fit into white plastic bases, and billboard sheet is folded in half and slid into slot in frame. Includes instruction sheet 71-2707-250. Type VI box. These billboards are larger and more modern-looking than their 2710 predecessors and incompatible with them. A large white frame has three narrow legs, and these plug into a long base. The small pegs on the frame legs are easily

Don't you just love that gigantic ice cream cone that rotates on the 12719 Animated Refreshment Stand? This popular accessory, cataloged by Lionel Trains Inc. for only a couple of years (1988–89), represents a revised version of the 128 Animated Newsstand from the postwar period.

	Exc	Mint

broken off if the billboard is disassembled, so once the frame is fastened to the base, operators should keep it that way. Six billboard signs are included in three double sheets; the sheets fold in half and are then inserted into slots in the billboard frame. For billboards, see 22A-B, 23A-B and 24A-B in the listings above.

CP

12719 ANIMATED REFRESHMENT STAND, 1988–89

Light gray base, white shed, light green roof, red and white lettering, checkerboard countertop. White-clad attendant moves to front, boy and girl figures rotate, and giant ice cream cone spins. With this accessory, LTI cleverly redesigned the newsstand into a corny but amusing operating device that has sold extremely well. It is powered by a belt-driven DC can motor instead of the old vibrator mechanism, but the motor drives the same set of operating levers as in the newsstand. A rotating ice cream cone takes the place of the dog and hydrant, while a teenage couple, quite realistically painted, revolves around on roller skates while enjoying ice cream treats. Meanwhile, a bald-headed attendant inside the stand moves forward to offer them another treat. As in the newsstand, a small lantern on the countertop illuminates when the accessory is operated. If the mechanism jams, it can be cured by carefully placing the upright spring inside the moving slot and rotating the mechanism gently until it is free. The accessory operates well at no more than 10 volts; most often jam-ups are caused by excessive voltage. The 12719 is a crowd-pleaser with a charm of its own. **Cross-references:** PW 128; ME 2308.

75   95

12722 ROADSIDE DINER WITH SMOKE, 1988–89

Light tan passenger car body mounted on dark gray base, red roof, black chimneys, black sign with white "LIONELVILLE DINER" lettering, illuminated, smoke from largest chimney, silhouettes in windows.

The 12722 Roadside Diner With Smoke adds interest to any layout. It was one of the first new accessories developed by engineers at Lionel Trains Inc.

Exc   Mint

The first roadside diner produced by Lionel since the prized prewar 442 landscaped model in 1938. Like that model, the diner itself is made from a passenger car body, in this case a 9500-style car. The interior is illuminated, and a small black chimney conceals a Seuthe-type smoke unit identical to the ones used in the LTI smoking cabooses and bunk cars. The body fits into a large base that can be landscaped, though it comes plain. Atop the roof stands a good-sized diner sign that attaches to two holes in the roof. **Cross-references:** ME 12771, 12802.

                                       40   **60**

12735 DIESEL HORN SHED, 1988–91

     Light tan house, dark brown roof and window edging, dark brown base, frosted window inserts, illuminated. Both this and a companion whistle shed were released in 1988 by LTI, but curiously the whistle shed has run much longer than this diesel shed. This accessory uses the more modern design of the postwar 114 rather than the old-fashioned 125 whistle shack. The postwar accessory used a bicycle horn and D-cell battery, but LTI replaced that mechanism with an electronic chipboard and a small speaker. The chipboard produces a different and more realistic sound than the 9-volt operated 2127 did. This time the colors used on the older models were reversed; the steam model follows the color pattern of the postwar diesel shed and vice versa. This probably has led to some confusion among older operators, who have long associated one color with one sound! The shed is illuminated, and this time the lighting is constant. **Cross-references:** PW 114; ME 12903.

                                         30   **40**

The 12735 Diesel Horn Shed (left) revives a useful accessory from the postwar era. For operators who like lots of sound, it makes a good companion to the 2125 Whistling Freight Shed (right).

Lionel Trains Inc. updated the useful freight shed with a whistle accessory in 1988 by housing the sound mechanism in a plastic structure that looks more up-to-date than the small shed Model Products Corp. had used for the 2126.

There's no mistaking this spectacular accessory from LTI. The 12767 Steam Clean and Wheel Grind Shop, introduced in 1994, featured three modules that could be used separately or combined to create a fascinating yard scene on a model railroad set in contemporary times. This photo shows a Santa Fe F3 on its journey through (left to right) the wheel grinding facility, wash rack, and steam cleaning facility.

	Exc	Mint

12737 WHISTLING FREIGHT SHED, 1988–97

Dark maroon house, white window edging, black roof, door, and base, illuminated. Introduced at the same time as the 12735, this whistle version of the modern postwar design has lasted much longer in the catalog, probably because there is always more of a need for whistles than diesel horns. (The majority of Lionel operators run steam trains, it is safe to say.) Additionally, the public may have liked the colors of this model better than the ones used for the 12735. It uses the same operating mechanism as the electronically operated 2126 in the older shed design. **Cross-reference: PW 118.**

	30	40

12761 ANIMATED BILLBOARD, 1990–91, 1993, and 1995

Red-brown base, light gray casing, on-off switch in back. Under normal voltage, billboard messages alter-

nate every 1½ seconds between "WELCOME TO LIONELVILLE" and "JOCKO SPORTING GOODS". This all-new design imitates the motor-driven billboards that change signs by means of rotating slats. In this case, the two billboard signs are made to change via a thermostatically operated mechanism that slides the slats instead of rotating them. An on-off switch can keep a constant display of one sign or the other. **Cross-reference: ME 12809.**

	25	30

12771 MOM'S ROADSIDE DINER, 1990–91

Dark brown base, light yellow dining car made from 9500-type passenger car body, light gray roof, red lettering, silhouettes in windows, black stack issues smoke, interior light, dark brown sign with white "MOM'S" lettering. This model of the roadside diner is essentially the same as the 12722, but it has different colors and lettering schemes. **Cross-references: ME 12722, 12771.**

	45	60

12767 STEAM CLEAN AND WHEEL GRIND SHOP, 1994–95

Consists of three modules (sold only as a set), each light gray plastic with bright red trim and yellow handrails. Module 1, the wash rack, has a light gray upper platform and tower supports, two large white cloth cylindrical wash spindles, a matching side shed with red window inserts and gray roof, and two black plastic floodlight towers with twin chromed reflectors. Module 2, the wheel grinding facility, is light gray with red trim and yellow ladders, with a white-coated attendant and one twin searchlight tower. Module 3, the steam cleaning facility, is light gray with red trim, but adds a dark gray single-dome tank with a painted attendant and clear plastic hose. The tank conceals a Seuthe-type smoke unit and has a twin-light searchlight tower and a flashing red light atop its platform.

This very large accessory is unique because it comes in three modules that can be set up in any order desired. As a locomotive passes through the first one, warning lights flash and the two cloth spindles rotate, simulating a rolling stock wash. There is, of course, no

water! As a locomotive files past the second module, flashing lights simulate the "sparks" thrown off from the wheel grinding process, which on prototype railroads restores true balance to the wheels and equalizes wear on them. The third module has a smoke unit, with a plastic hose emanating smoke as a locomotive passes through it to simulate a steam cleaning. Each module has upright twin floodlight towers (the wash module has two). This is a versatile arrangement that makes for an active maintenance yard.

275   325

12802 CHAT & CHEW ROADSIDE DINER, 1992–95

Dark red 9500-style passenger car body with smoke unit, interior illumination, window silhouettes, and gold lettering, mounted on a bright yellow-green base; two 12802 Highway Lights in front base corners, black "CHAT AND CHEW DINER" sign atop roof with gold edge and lettering. This diner is essentially the same as its two LTI predecessors, except for one notable addition: In each front corner of the base, a 12804

Concerned about patrons of its diner having to park their cars in a darkened lot, LTI installed a pair of 12804 Highway Lights on the base and thereby created the 12802 Chat & Chew Roadside Diner, which it cataloged from 1992 through 1995.

Always looking to diversify Lionel's line of accessories, LTI developed the 12889 Operating Windmill, which it cataloged for the first time in 1995.

Highway Light has been installed. The two lampposts make a bright and attractive addition to this accessory. **Cross-references:** ME 12722, 12771.

50   60

12809 ANIMATED BILLBOARD, 1992–93

Red-brown base, small black on-off switch, gray frame, signs as described for 12761. Frame and base colors are identical to the earlier model, but the signs are "LOOK, LISTEN, LIVE" with F3 diesel and crossing gate and smaller-lettered "Always Observe Crossing Signals" with large red sign "MILK" and diving woman figure; "America's Health Kick." **Cross-reference:** ME 12761.

30   35

12889 OPERATING WINDMILL, 1995–97

Black plastic simulated wood base, gray-painted tower structure, black balance fin and motor atop black motor base, large multiple-bladed white plastic fan rotates by direct drive from motor. This new design by LTI has a metal girder structure that appears to be similar to the one used for the oil derricks. Mounted atop the structure is a small can motor that spins the blades; a balance vane is attached to the motor. The top also swivels, according to the catalog. For the electrical connections, a metal rod is inserted into the base and extends to the motor structure. That's a reversal from the modern-era wiring scheme for the similar rotating beacon.

CP

12898 FLAG POLE KIT, 1995–97

Red-brown base, American flag, red "LIONEL" triangular pennant with white lettering, string for attachment to white flagpole. The little square sponge pieces of previous versions are absent from the catalog illustration. Identical to the 2320, except the Lionel pennant is red and not blue. **Cross-references:** PW 89; ME 2320.

CP

12903 DIESEL HORN SHED, 1995–97

Red-brown base, black shed with white "LIONEL" and circle-L logo on signboard below window, doors and windows outlined in white, interior illumination, opaque window inserts, dark gray roof. Identical in operation to the 12735, but this version features new, bolder colors. This lends credence to the idea that the previous version was discontinued because its colors were not attractive enough to sell as well as the 12737 Whistling Freight Shed version. **Cross-references:** PW 114; ME 12735.

CP

12962 PASSENGER SERVICE CENTER WITH STEAM WHISTLE, 1997

Catalog shows red-brown base, yellow building with red striping and paper inserts depicting phone banks, etc., illuminated inside as before, silver-painted roof. Can motor-driven steam air whistle mechanism as on previous models. The catalog shows this to be essentially a redecorated 12737 with (as the catalog states) "pay phones with data ports, ATM, send-a-fax stations and baggage claim." Operationally it is the same steam whistle shed as its predecessors. It seems curious that Lionel would market such a "modern" version of this accessory and keep the obsolete steam whistle rather than installing a modern diesel horn! **Cross-references:** PW 118; ME 12737.

CP

8

BUILDING KITS

Some unusual railroad laws passed by states over the years:

> *Positively no shooting of pheasants or cattle from train.*
> —Pennsylvania

> *All male passengers must assist crew in shoveling snow or pushing if necessary.*
> —Pennsylvania

> *When two trains approach each other at a crossing, they shall both come to a full stop and neither shall start up until the other has gone.*
> —Kansas

> *A dog shall be carried on the cowcatcher of all trains. The dog is necessary to put to flight cattle obstructing the track.* —Washington

> *Children can not be employed to run trains.*
> —Montana

INTRODUCTION

Ever since people miniaturized the railway (soon after the real ones emerged), they have desired to grace their layouts with buildings of all sorts. Sometimes—perhaps most of the time—operators would avail themselves of ready-made building kits that they could glue together and perhaps customize with a little paint. Modern plastic kits made this chore relatively easy, since all parts were precut to size. However, wood kits were more of a challenge because of the exact sanding needed. Sometimes building kits were made out of stiff cardstock preprinted and ready for tab-and-slot assembly.

Of course, for real individualists there were other ways to get those buildings and make them unique. Most builders of model railroads know about the fine arts of *kitbashing* and *scratchbuilding*. Kitbashing is a technique in which parts of several ready-made kits are recombined into an entirely new building. A common example of this is the Plasticville Apartment Building; the kit contains only one story, but these stories can be combined from many kits until a railroader has a mid-rise or even high-rise apartment building gracing his layout. Scratchbuilding is just what its name implies—building a structure "from scratch." Many years ago an HO scale modeler named E. L. Moore became legendary for his ingenious scratchbuilt structures. One of his best buildings was a firecracker factory with twin towers made in the shape of huge Roman candles. Moore tore a hole in the roof and inserted the top half of a human figure, explaining that "Johnny Jones just couldn't resist sneakin' a smoke now and then!"

In the postwar years, Lionel realized that building kits would be highly desirable if they were sold under the Lionel name. Having no in-house expertise in the matter, Lionel contracted with Bachmann, the makers of Plasticville, to supply building kits for the Lionel catalogs. A fine variety of these kits was marketed, and many are highly prized if they are accompanied by their original boxes.

When General Mills took over Lionel in late 1969, the new owners recognized the need for buildings and structures to be put together by consumers. One odd approach was to place house- and factory-shaped pieces of Styrofoam packaging into train sets in 1971; this was the famous and short-lived Foam Village Packaging by Myco. Consumers were to paint the plain Styrofoam blocks so they would look like houses. It wasn't a successful technique and was soon abandoned. Another approach that same year was to market three sets of specially commissioned Plasticville assortments under the

Lionel name. These were the Cross Country, Whistle Stop, and Alamo Junction sets. The Plasticville items in these sets were the same as those Plasticville itself marketed, except that in many cases the colors were molded in reverse of the usual practice. For example, if the Plasticville water tank had a gray tank and a brown roof, the Lionel version would have a brown tank and a gray roof. Many examples of the Plasticville structures made for Lionel are found in marbled plastic —a sign that scrap plastic was used for their molding. This too was just a stopgap approach.

Fortunately for the new Lionel, General Mills had control of an excellent model manufacturing company, Model Products Corporation (MPC). By early 1973, MPC had begun to turn out a diversified, high-quality line of stations, towers, engine houses, and commercial buildings. These kits featured thick, durable styrene plastic pieces that were precolored and ready to glue into good-looking, permanent structures for the layout. The most spectacular of these was the Rico Station, modeled after a famous rococo station in Rico, Colorado. It had every Victorian filigree, finial, and gingerbread piece of the original and looked great on any layout. All these building kits sold very well. Some collectors have speculated that the source of them was the European Pola Company, which had made quality building kits for many years. However, it must be said that MPC certainly had the expertise to come up with these kits all by itself.

The success of the first kits marketed in Type II boxes encouraged Fundimensions to expand the line into very large and very small structures for any building need. These ranged from the very small but well detailed barrel loader buildings to massive grain and coal elevator kits in huge boxes. Unassembled kits in these mid-1970s Type II boxes are extremely difficult to find today. New versions were marketed in Type III boxes throughout the Fundimensions Era.

Lionel Trains Inc. took over where Fundimensions left off. Not only were the old kits brought out in new colors but new designs were forthcoming. Brand new to the line during the current production year are a factory, maintenance shed and truck loading dock. Lionel layout builders have a tremendous choice of both old and new designs, and all these buildings look good on a layout. These kits give the look and feel of a miniature world in full operation, and perhaps that is why they are of such importance. The illusion of reality would not be there without convincing structures, and Lionel has done an excellent job of providing those in the modern era.

Note: With building kits, "Mint" condition assumes that the kit is complete and comes unassembled in its original box, preferably with the parts still sealed in their packing bags. Assembled kits are assumed to be in "Like New" or "Excellent" condition.

2175 SANDY ANDY GRAVEL LOADER, 1976–79

Light brown structure, dark brown roof and base, gray plastic girders, light brown ore cart. Difficult to find in intact, working condition; even harder to find as an unassembled kit. This building kit was not only a spectacular sight when it was assembled, it also operated quite convincingly, although sometimes temperamentally. The top of the silo is loaded with coal or ore. This little cart is attached to a string with a weight. When a lever holding the weight is released, the weight brings the cart to the top of incline, where it pushes against a lever that uncovers a hole releasing the coal into the cart. When the weight of the coal overcomes the brass weight on the line attached to the cart, it travels down girders and is tripped into a chute that unloads the coal into a waiting car or bin. The cycle then begins again. The action is difficult to adjust properly, but its activity is clever and delightful when the loader works as it should. This accessory came in a modified Type III box with nonverbal instructions, a concession by Lionel to a modern, multilingual society. **Cross-reference:** ME 12712.

40	**60**

2709 RICO STATION, 1981–95

Large plastic kit measuring 22" long and 9" wide, came in different colors than the 2797; it looks good thanks to ample detail; though all versions in all colors have been popular, the 2797 is the one most prized by collectors. This impressive station kit has been a staple of the modern-era building kit lineup since its introduction in 1976. It features every design element of the classic Victorian station in Rico, Colorado, right down to the gingerbread decor along the top of the roof and around the colorful cupola. When LTI took over production of this kit in 1987, a few color changes were made, but the kit has been marketed with the same number to the present. **Cross-reference:** ME 2797.

(A) 1981–86, dark brown base, main roof and window and door inserts, gray cupola roof and chimneys, light tan station walls, came in Type III packaging.

20	**30**

(B) 1987–95, same as (A), but base and chimneys are light gray, main roof is dark gray, window, door and trim inserts are medium brown, came in Type VI packaging.

CP

The 2719 Watchman's Shanty, shown in this cata-log illustration from 1987, resembled a signal tower that Bachmann manufactured.

Exc Mint

2718 BARREL PLATFORM, 1977–84

Plastic kit includes figure, barrels, tools, lamp, ladder, and building, measures 4" x 4" x 3½"; gray base and platform, brown plat-form supports, red-brown shed, dark gray door and window inserts, dark brown roof, Type III packaging. This small Fundi-mensions kit, a good seller, features a small shed atop a platform on stilts with a figure, several tools, and little plastic barrels. Its LTI reissue features new colors and a new number. **Cross-reference:** ME 12718.

5 7

2719 WATCHMAN'S SHANTY, 1977–87

Bright green base and steps, light brown structure, dark gray window and door inserts, light gray roof; kit measures 7" x 4" x 4½" and comes with watchman and dog figures. The name of this accessory is mis-leading; it is a signal tower similar to the one produced by Bachmann for many years. Lionel's version has a different steps ar-rangement and a more pointed roof. **Cross-reference:** ME 12733.

5 7

2720 LUMBER SHED: 1977–84 and 1987

Light green structure, gray roofs, light tan lumber stacks and cutting table, light gray base; kit measures 4" high, 6" long, and 3½" wide and comes with worker, shed, table, lumber, tools, ladder; Type III packag-ing. This is an open shed with a slanted roof, worker figure, and stacks of lumber. Other details include a sawing table at the build-ing's side and ladders. It kept the same colors during its brief LTI revival in 1987 and was replaced by the 12705. **Cross-reference:** ME 12705.

5 7

The 2720 Lumber Shed returned to the line in 1987. This catalog photograph shows the finished struc-ture and the details that came with the kit.

The 2783 Freight Station Kit, cataloged by Fundimensions between 1981 and 1985, built up into an impressive and realistic structure.

	Exc	Mint

2721 LOG LOADING MILL, 1978

Red plastic kit, manual operation: pressing a lever causes plastic log to be released and roll down ramp. This one-color kit was produced for the no. 1862 Workin' On The Railroad Logging Empire set and included in various uncataloged versions. It was not available for separate sale, except during LTI era as the 12774. **Cross-reference:** ME 12774.

3   5

2722 BARREL LOADER, 1978–79

Green plastic kit, manual operation, worker pushes barrel down a chute. This one-color kit came in the no. 1862 Workin' On The Railroad Logging Empire set and included in various uncataloged versions. It was not available for separate sale. **Cross-references:** ME 2723, 12706.

3   5

2723 BARREL LOADER, 1984

Brown plastic kit, manual operation, worker pushes barrel down a chute. This one-color kit is iden-

	Exc	Mint

tical to the 2722, except for its color, which was changed to match the brown and red tones of the no. 1403 Redwood Valley Express set in which it came. It was not offered for separate sale. **Cross-reference:** ME 2722.

3   5

2729 WATER TOWER BUILDING KIT, 1985

Orange-brown pump house with gray door and window insert, light tan base, gray ladder, green tower support frame, light tan tank, gray spout, green tank roof. Pictured in the 1985 Traditional Catalogue, but canceled from dealer order sheets in September 1985. Water tower kit in same colors released in 1987 as 12711. This kit would have been virtually identical to the 2789, except for a gray roof instead of a green one. However, it was canceled, possibly as a casualty of the Mexican move recovery then taking place. **Cross-references:** ME 2789, 12711.

Not manufactured

2783 FREIGHT STATION KIT, 1981–85

Light brown sides, dark brown platform, doors and windows, light gray roof, brick red chimney. This was

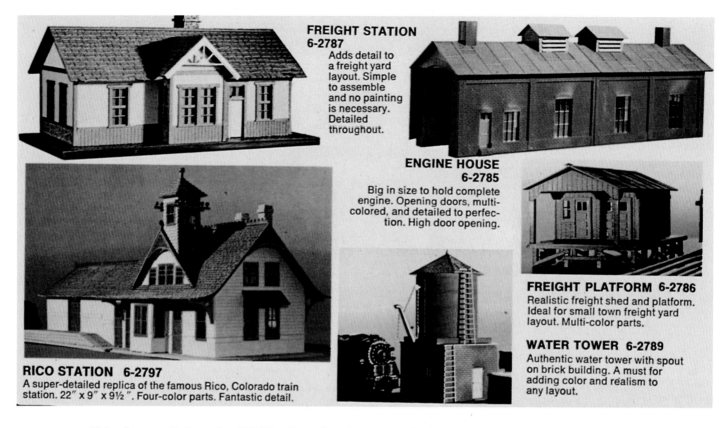

FREIGHT STATION 6-2787
Adds detail to a freight yard layout. Simple to assemble and no painting is necessary. Detailed throughout.

ENGINE HOUSE 6-2785
Big in size to hold complete engine. Opening doors, multi-colored, and detailed to perfection. High door opening.

FREIGHT PLATFORM 6-2786
Realistic freight shed and platform. Ideal for small town freight yard layout. Multi-color parts.

WATER TOWER 6-2789
Authentic water tower with spout on brick building. A must for adding color and realism to any layout.

RICO STATION 6-2797
A super-detailed replica of the famous Rico, Colorado train station. 22" x 9" x 9½". Four-color parts. Fantastic detail.

This photograph from the 1976 Lionel catalog shows several of the realistic and colorful building kits that were included in the line during the mid-1970s.

	Exc	Mint

the second Fundimensions issue of the traditional freight station; it was similar to the 2787 except for color changes and Type III packaging. **Cross-references:** ME 2787, PW 12734.

	7	10

2784 FREIGHT PLATFORM, 1981–87 and 1989

Dark green building with dark gray door, window inserts, and roof atop medium green platform and supports, Type III packaging. This is the second Fundimensions issue of a rather rustic-looking small-town freight storage shed. Note the curious numbering of the later Fundimensions kits with lower numbers than their earlier counterparts. **Cross-references:** ME 2786, 12773.

	6	10

2785 ENGINE HOUSE, 1974–77

Large, long single-track structure with red-brown simulated brick walls, bright green window inserts, dark gray swinging doors and roof with two smoke

escape clerestories, red-brown chimneys, Type II packaging. When found in its original box, this is among the most prized Fundimensions kits. Similar kits have been produced in the past few years, both in single- and double-track versions, by Pola, International Hobby Corp., and other firms. **Cross-references:** ME 12710, 12897.

	40	50

2786 FREIGHT PLATFORM, 1974–77

Dark green building with dark gray roof and chimney, medium gray doors and window inserts, dark brown platform and supports. The first Fundimensions issue of the country-style freight platform, it is almost identical to the 2784 except for the packaging and base color. **Cross-references:** ME 2784, 12773.

	6	10

2787 FREIGHT STATION, 1974–77 and 1983

Yellow-brown walls with light brown window and door inserts, light brown paneling along bottom edge of

Among the most prized of the early structure kits marketed by Fundimensions is the 2788 Coaling Station, which was part of the Lionel line from 1975 to 1977.

	Exc	Mint

walls, light gray base, gable support and chimney, medium green roof. This first edition of the freight station kit was portrayed in the 1974 catalog with the sign "HAMLET", which might certainly have been appropriate. However, the kit did not include any such sign. **Cross-references:** ME 2783, 12734.

	7	**10**

2788 COALING STATION, 1975–77

Light gray base, tan main building with brown window inserts, gray roof and coal chute, green side building with gray roof, brick red sub-building, brown trestle support. A flip of a lever sends coal into a wait-

	Exc	Mint

ing car through an overhead chute. Type II packaging. Along with the engine house, early Rico station, and grain elevator, this is one of the most highly prized of all the early building kits. Its large and imposing stance distinguishes it on any layout. **Cross-references:** ME 12736, 12904.

	40	**50**

2789 WATER TOWER, 1975–77 and 1980

Light gray base, ladders, window and door inserts, light gray roof, brick red support building, light tan tank structure, light gray spout and chain, Type II packaging; somewhat hard to find. In slightly smaller

The 2789 Water Tower didn't make much of a splash when it was introduced in 1975. That may explain why this kit is somewhat difficult to find today.

CROSS COUNTRY SET
Included 17½" long Trestle Bridge. Watchman's Shanty with tool shed and Crossing Gate, 5 Telephone Poles, 12 Railroad Signs. Ideal for layouts accented with miniature cars. Easy to assemble.
No. 6-2791

WHISTLE STOP SET
Double track Signal Bridge with red, yellow and green signal lights. Watchman's Shanty with Tool Shed and crossing gate. Freight Loading Platform with baggage accessories. Easy to assemble. Five Telephone Poles.
No. 6-2792

ALAMO JUNCTION SET
Includes 2 story Switch Tower, Water Tank with spout, Watchman's Shanty with Crossing Gate and Tool Shed, and five Telephone Poles. Easy to assemble.
No. 6-2793

The 2791 Cross Country Set, 2792 Whistle Stop Set, and 2793 Alamo Junction Set were nicely depicted in Lionel's catalog for 1971. Each set came with a terrific assortment of structures and details.

The 2792 Whistle Stop Set provided plenty of enjoyment for kids in 1970 and 1971. This assortment of Plasticville structure kits gave young operators much of what they needed to build an interesting layout.

	Exc	Mint

form, this water tower kit resembled many European models of American water tanks produced for larger scales. **Cross-references:** ME 2729, 12711.

	20	25

2790 BUILDING KIT ASSORTMENT, 1978–83

Twelve building kits in master carton as described individually. Dealer assortment that included four 2718 Barrel Platforms, four 2719 Watchman's Shanties, and four 2720 Lumber Sheds. **Cross-references:** ME 2718, 2719, 2720 (components).

NRS

2791 CROSS COUNTRY SET, 1970–71

Five telephone poles, twelve railroad signs, watchman's shanty with crossing gate; 17¼" black trestle

	Exc	Mint

bridge; contents wrapped in brown paper inside Type I box. This and the 2792 and 2793 sets featured Plasticville pieces supplied to Fundimensions by Bachmann. Often the components can be found in reversed color schemes from the standard Plasticville production, and sometimes they are made of "marbled" plastic. **Cross-references:** PW 981, 984, 988.

	30	40

2792 LAYOUT STARTER PAK, 1980–84

Assortment of building kits and scenic items packaged in Type III box (most likely); see individual entries for descriptions. The items included a snap-together extension bridge kit, a barrel platform kit, a lumber shed kit, ten telephone poles, fourteen road signs, five billboards, and a Track Layout Book. This assortment of kits and scenery was intended for public purchase, not as a dealer's item. **Cross-references:** ME

The 2793 Alamo Junction Set, much like its companion, the 2792, contained a variety of Plasticville structures that youngsters could use to make their train set more fun to play with. The colors on the different buildings could vary.

	Exc	Mint
2717, 2718, 2720, 2180, 2181, 2710, 2951 (components).	**10**	**25**

2792 WHISTLE STOP SET, 1970–71

Assortment of Plasticville building kits: signal bridge, watchman's shanty with crossing gate, freight loading platform with baggage accessories, and five light brown telephone poles. Packaged in a Type I box, this set contained standard Plasticville structures, sometimes cast in reverse colors from regular Plasticville production or even in marbled plastic. **Cross-references:** PW 981, 984, 988.

30   40

	Exc	Mint

2793 ALAMO JUNCTION SET, 1970–71

Assortment of Plasticville building kits: water tank with gray base, framework, and roof, brown tank; switch tower with brown base, steps, roof, and doors, gray sides; watchman's shanty with gray base, roof, and windows, brown building, black and white crossing gate; five light brown telephone poles. It came packaged in a Type I box. **Cross-references:** PW 981, 984, 988.

30   40

2796 GRAIN ELEVATOR, 1976–77

Large tan building measuring 16" high, 16" long, 13" wide, with dark brown roofs, window and door

Both collectors and operators like the 2797 Rico Station, one of the most popular of the building kits that have become staples of the modern-era line of accessories. This early version is more difficult to find than the later 2709.

Exc Mint

inserts, ramps and ladders, light tan roof support similar to coal loader kit holds roof across tracks, red and white checkerboard band around building just below second-level roofs, yellow-brown base, Type III packaging. This huge kit, the largest of all the modern-era models, was introduced in late 1975 through a special dealer flyer; only the first Rico Station was granted such an introduction. Along with that station, the early coaling tower and the first Sandy Andy, this is among the most desirable of all the building kits. Just imagine putting this kit alongside the new Operating Windmill for a great farm setting! **Cross-reference:** ME 12726.

60   75

Exc Mint

2797 RICO STATION, 1976–77

Yellow-brown building (a little darker than the 2709) with dark brown doors, window inserts and "gingerbread," dark gray roofs, cupola and chimneys. The earliest version of the Rico Station was not much different from its much more common successor, but this version is difficult to find unassembled in its original box. The most noticeable difference is that the base of this version is medium gray rather than the later dark brown. **Cross-reference:** ME 2709.

40   60

Exc   Mint

12705 LUMBER SHED, 1988–97

Black structure, black base, dark tan awnings, light tan roof supports, light tan simulated lumber stacks, unpainted gray figure. This LTI-produced lumber shed is identical to its predecessors except for its colors and Type VI packaging. **Cross-reference:** ME 2720.

CP

12706 BARREL LOADER BUILDING, 1987–97

All-gray or all-red-brown platform, barrels, figure, barrel chute, and shack; manual turn of lever sends

Exc   Mint

barrel out chute into car. This one-color barrel loader appears identical to the older kits included in the Workin' On The Railroad sets, but it was offered for separate sale in Type VI packaging. It has been issued in two colors: gray or red-brown. **Cross-references:** ME 2722, 2723.

CP

12710 ENGINE HOUSE, 1987–91

Brick red building measuring 20½" x 6⅛" x 7⅛", black doors and windows, gray roof. This was LTI's first reissue of the scarce Fundimensions model. It was

The 12710 Engine House, cataloged from 1987–91, was one of the largest building kits available from Lionel Trains Inc. Looking counterclockwise, the 12710 is pictured with the 12706 Barrel Loading Building (which featured manual operation), 12705 Lumber Shed (as reissued in different colors), and 2784 Freight Platform in the 1989 Toy Fair Edition of the LTI catalog.

In 1987, Lionel Trains Inc. revived the 2175 Sandy Andy Gravel Loader as the 12712 Automatic Ore Loader. The new accessory featured different colors and handled ore rather than sand.

	Exc	Mint

identical to its predecessor except for its colors and Type VI packaging. **Cross-references:** ME 2785, 12897.

	25	30

12711 WATER TOWER KIT, 1987–95

Light tan base, brown (not red-brown) support structure, light tan water tank and rack support, dark gray roof, light gray spout, chain, ladder, and door and window supports. This LTI issue of the water tower kit was not only a revival of the 2789 in different colors, but also a direct duplication of the 2729 from the 1985

	Exc	Mint

catalog, which was never produced. **Cross-references:** ME 2729, 2789.

		CP

12712 AUTOMATIC ORE LOADER, 1987–88

Bright blue base, roofs, and chute roof, yellow elevator tower and structure, gray tower supports, yellow ore car tracks, gray ore car; comes with ore and gray dumping bin. Identical in function to the 2175 Sandy Andy, except for new colors and Type VI packaging, but also supplied with ore instead of sand; the ore appears

Two more stalwart members of the LTI line of building kits were the 12711 Water Tower and the 12718 Barrel Shed, both of which were easily assembled into neat-looking structures to enhance O and O27 gauge layouts.

Exc   Mint

to make the device work better, though it is still temperamental. See 2175 for description of this accessory's action. **Cross-reference:** ME 2175.

35   45

12718 BARREL SHED KIT, 1987–97

Earliest versions all light tan; later ones have light tan base and platform, dark brown platform supports, tan figure, white barrels, white house with dark gray roof, window inserts and door. This LTI kit is identical to its Fundimensions predecessor, except for colors and Type VI packaging. **Cross-reference:** ME 2718.

CP

12726 GRAIN ELEVATOR, 1988–91, 1994–97

Light yellow building sides and roof support, brown window inserts, light gray roof pieces and ramp, black platform; it lacks the checkerboard red and white band of the 2796. Identical to Fundimensions model, except for colors and Type VI packaging. **Cross-reference:** ME 2796.

CP

12733 WATCHMAN'S SHANTY, 1988–97

Dark red-brown house, black roof, light gray steps and stairway, light gray base, dark brown doors and

Exc   Mint

window inserts. Identical to the earlier model, except for colors and Type VI packaging. More properly called a switch tower than a watchman's shanty, this accessory bears a resemblance to the Plasticville switch tower produced for many years. **Cross-reference:** ME 2719.

CP

12734 PASSENGER/FREIGHT STATION, 1989–97

Light brown building, brick-red roof, gray chimney, dark gray base, medium brown window and door inserts; early production had lighter gray base and green window and door inserts. This station has only slight differences in colors from its predecessors. Note, however, that two color schemes have been produced with the same number. Type VI packaging. **Cross-references:** ME 2783, 2787.

CP

12736 COALING STATION, 1988–91

Red-brown lower tower, dark tan housing, light gray roof, dark gray tipple structure and housing, light brown doors, window inserts and shed roof girder support. This LTI version of the coaling tower was carried through only 1991; the kit was reissued with a new number and new colors in 1995. The 12736 is identical to the 2788, except for colors and Type VI packaging. **Cross-references:** ME 2788, 12904.

20   30

Exc   Mint

12750 CRANE KIT, 1989–91

Yellow crane and cab body, black crane and superstructure, swiveling cab and operating hook, Type VI packaging. Crane is modeled after the Harnischfeger kits of the postwar era; it is almost identical to the crane that came with the 9157 Chesapeake & Ohio flatcar in 1975. **Cross-references:** PW 6828-100; ME 12900.

                    10   12

12751 SHOVEL KIT, 1989–91

Yellow cab, black shovel and superstructure, gray rubber treads. Shovel opens, closes, raises, and lowers by hand. Power shovel owes its lineage to Harnischfeger kits of the postwar years; it is nearly identical to the shovel that came with the 9158 Penn Central flatcar in 1975. **Cross-references:** PW 6827-100; ME 12901.

                    10   12

12773 FREIGHT PLATFORM KIT, 1990–97

Early version had red base and building, light gray doors and windows, dark gray roof; later one had dark brown base and building, dark gray roof, doors and window inserts. The early version of this kit came in very bright colors that later were toned down without a change of number. It is otherwise identical to its predecessors, down to the rustic look. Type VI packaging. **Cross-references:** ME 2784, 2786.

                    CP

12774 LUMBER LOADER KIT, 1990–97

Tan structure, light tan roof, four logs. As with many LTI reissues of Fundimensions kits, it is identical to predecessor except

The 12734 Passenger/Freight Station and the 12726 Grain Elevator made outstanding additions to any Lionel layout, no matter what its size.

The detailed structure kits available from Lionel in recent years, including the 12718 Barrel Shed (shown on the left after being painted for the 1991 catalog) represent quite an improvement from the unpainted Styrofoam buildings such as the one on the right that Model Products Corp. offered not long after it began producing the Lionel line.

                                        Exc   Mint

for color and Type VI packaging. However, the Fun-dimensions version was included in the Workin' On The Railroad Logging Empire sets and never sold separately. A flip of a plastic lever sends logs down a chute into a waiting car. **Cross-reference:** ME 2721.

                                              CP

12884 TRUCK LOADING DOCK, 1995–97

Open air shed with slanted roof; dark brown arched girder supports and platform, dark gray floor and extension ramp top, light gray roof; accessory measures 11½" x 7½" x 5½". It made sense for LTI to

                                        Exc   Mint

produce this kit, since it invested heavily in the production of tractors and trailers, not to mention several intermodal container kits and separate frames that allow operators to create any design possible. The shed is also useful with the big intermodal cranes and TOFC (Trailer On Flat Car) articulated rolling stock pieces of recent years.

                                              CP

12897 ENGINE HOUSE, 1995–97

Light gray building walls and chimneys, dark brown door and window inserts, dark brown end doors

The engineers at LTI cleverly designed some of the brand-new building kits to operate. One favorite is the 12774 Lumber Loader Kit, shown in action for the 1991 catalog.

Exc   Mint

and clerestories, dark gray roof. Most engine houses on the market, including two previous Lionel kits, use a basic brick-red color scheme. This reissue features a new gray and dark brown scheme that should meet wide acceptance from operators and collectors. **Cross-references:** ME 2785, 12710.

CP

12900 CRANE KIT, 1995–97

Bright orange driver's cab, crane housing and wheel hubs, dark gray crane boom, support stanchions, and superstructure. This crane kit is identical to its predecessors, except for color scheme. No manufacturer identification marks, but it resembles Harnischfeger crane of postwar years. **Cross-references:** PW 6828-100; ME 12750.

CP

12901 SHOVEL KIT, 1995–97

Bright orange cab, dark gray shovel and boom and support stanchion, black undercarriage with black rubber traction treads. Like the 12900, this shovel is designed to match its postwar and LTI predecessors. No manufacturer identification marks, but it resembles

Exc   Mint

Harnischfeger shovel of postwar years. **Cross-references:** PW 6827-100; ME 12751.   **CP**

12904 COALING STATION, 1995–97

Light tan base, bright red lower story with white window and door inserts, dark gray side storage bin and roof, white support girders, black upper story with white window inserts and light gray roof pieces. Coaling station resembles its predecessors, but has brighter colors. **Cross-references:** ME 2788, 12736.

CP

12905 FACTORY, 1995–97

Red building with light tan large doors and window inserts at loading dock half, light tan loading dock structure, bright green gutters and downspouts, bright green window inserts, doors and chimney on storage half of building and side shed, medium gray roof with light tan chimneys. It isn't the replica of the Lionel factory many operators and collectors would like, but this new design should be a useful adjunct to road-rail transfer facilities on a layout. Note that the same design is used for the 12906 with different arrangements for doors and walls.   **CP**

12906 MAINTENANCE SHED, 1995–97

Bright orange simulated brickwork structure, large opening without doors at one end, bright green large window inserts, gutters and downspouts, medium gray roof with light tan chimneys; side shed follows same color pattern. Same general design as used with 12905, but the walls of the building are different. One end of the structure has a large opening without doors (unlike the engine houses). This structure is meant to be placed at the end of a siding so rolling stock can be wheeled inside for maintenance.

CP

12931 ELECTRICAL SUBSTATION BUILDING KIT, 1996–97

Red-brick platform base and walls, dark gray opening doors and window inserts, light green roof with gray trim and skylight frame, light gray platform extension. Size 7¾" x 7⅞" x 9" when assembled; platform ramp extends another 6¾". This is a well-scaled kit in the form of a brick building; it has the authentic look of a power station from the early years of this century. One surprise: it is made and packaged in Denmark! **Cross-references:** None; new model.

CP

12951 AIRPLANE HANGAR BUILDING KIT, 1997

Dark gray hangar building and doors, light gray window inserts, translucent clear plastic roof. Measures 10⅝" x 9¾" x 4⅝" when assembled. All Lionel operators who used the old Plasticville airport hangar on their layouts will be pleased to see this Lionel alternative. The catalog specifies that it is made to accommodate the Lionel Beechcraft planes found on the many flatcars Lionel has issued in recent years. Its doors open and close by sliding motion rather than the Plasticville model's hanging door. **Cross-references:** None; new model.

CP

12952 BIG "L" DINER BUILDING KIT, 1997

Chromed silver diner structure, printed window inserts with venetian blinds and "customers," large "LIONEL DINER" sign atop building with Circle L logo. This is the first original diner of any kind Lionel has issued. Previous versions had always featured converted passenger car bodies, like the prewar 442 landscaped diner done with a 600-series passenger car body and the recent roadside diners with smoke, which used 9500-series passenger car bodies. The catalog illustration shows a chromed diner with a definite fifties look. **Cross-references:** None; new model.

CP

12953 LINEX GASOLINE TANK (TALL), 1997

Medium gray plastic cylinder with simulated steel plating; orange and yellow Linex pressure-sensitive sticker supplied; measures 6" in diameter by 6⅜" in height. After all the aftermarket tank structures available to the Lionel operator, it is somewhat relieving to see Lionel finally follow suit. The catalog suggests painting the plastic cylinder a bright silver and then applying the bright Linex pressure-adhesive sign to it. **Cross-references:** None; new model.

CP

12954 LINEX GASOLINE OIL TANK (WIDE), 1997

Same as 12953, except measures 7⅜" in diameter by 4" in height. Same features as 12953, but in a different configuration. **Cross-references:** None; new model.

CP

9

ROAD VEHICLES

The railroads must provide a service tailored to the customers' needs of moving commodities and merchandise cheaply—without damage or excessive handling, and with efficient speed from origin to destination. The customer would not adapt his needs to what the railroad would supply. . . . The long silver TOFC trains . . . cut carloading and handling costs to the bone, and brought back tons and tons of merchandise traffic that otherwise would have been lost to the highway.
—Robert S. Carper, *American Railroads in Transition*

INTRODUCTION

In one respect, real railroads and Lionel trains were exactly alike: both were slow to adapt to new, cooperative means of hauling freight. However, once they did recognize the need for intermodal ventures, they did so with a vengeance. Joshua Lionel Cowen often socialized with railroading people, and legend has it that he chastised many rail officials for being stodgy and unimaginative, just as if he himself were a railroad president. Even in the 1920s, Lionel produced LCL (Less than Carload Lot) metal containers to fit aboard the 200- and 500-series gondolas of the Standard gauge era. That was more than many real railroads were willing to do for customers.

During the 1950s, the new Interstate Highway System threatened freight traffic on the railroads as never before. The more enlightened railroads came up with methods to transport road trailers from terminal to terminal atop specially designed flatcars. The reasoning was that it made more sense to cooperate with highway transportation than to compete with it. The new TOFC (Trailer On Flat Car) system was extremely successful; it led to even better container-shipping cars and other specialized rolling stock that made railroads efficient shippers of bulk commodities once again. Lionel was right on top of these developments; in 1955 the firm modified its 6511-type flatcar to carry two freight trailers. These trailers had an old-fashioned look to them with their rounded ends and corrugated sides, but at least Lionel was moving in the right direction. At about the same time, Lionel introduced a manually operated trailer-loading accessory. However, Cowen was near retiring and selling his company, and Lionel's new management was anything but forward-looking. Therefore, trailer-railroad shipping on the Lionel Lines was a side show at best.

Recognizing the popularity of the TOFC car, Fundimensions made it one of its first revivals in 1970 with a Northern Pacific model that retained the old-fashioned corrugated-side trailers. Soon the trailers lost their corrugated sides so that bright, new graphics could be applied to the trailers. The TOFC cars sold well and were produced in variety, but no one at Fundimensions did anything about associated accessories or road vehicles until 1977. In that year the firm brought out two inexpensive starter sets with many play pieces, the Workin' On The Railroad sets. These included one or more of three plastic tractor units, two with a yellow slab-sided open trailer and one with a blue flat trailer without sides. It was a start, but Fundimensions never tried to supply a truly modern intermodal facility for O gauge operators.

That situation changed immediately when Lionel Trains Inc. took over production of the line in 1987. First of all, the trailers on the flatcars were redesigned with square ends. This made them look contemporary, though they still were too small. Another step taken was the production of a single-trailer Burlington Northern TOFC car, and this was a herald of things to come because the trailer had a separate body and metal frame. However, the accessory that really forced the issue was the mammoth Intermodal Crane, cataloged in 1987 and 1988 and scheduled for production again in 1997. It could load and unload trailers from TOFC cars as part of a complete intermodal terminal.

The older, short trailers were too small to look realistic with this accessory, so operators demanded bigger, realistic tractor-trailer units.

LTI's answer to this demand was revolutionary because it created a new and highly collectible group of well-made accessories that were inexpensive yet realistic. These were the Lionel die-cast tractor-trailer units, made in Macao to Lionel's standards. The first one, a bright orange Lionel tractor and trailer, was delayed for almost a year, but once these items began to be made, LTI couldn't produce them fast enough. So far, more than thirty-five different models of these sturdy, well-detailed road vehicles have been manufactured, and the trend shows no signs of letting up. In fact, these units sold so well that many American oil companies began to market their own units, not to mention such diverse firms as the Dunkin' Donuts restaurant chain. Other toy train manufacturers have marketed somewhat larger tractors and trailers, and the second half of the intermodal shipping pair has become a fixture on many a layout.

Lionel has also marketed assortments of three containers (five sets so far) that fit the same frames and flatcars. Even the trailer frames are available for separate sale; therefore, collectors are likely to observe LTI's tractors and trailers in just about any combination. These containers may also be seen, with or without frames, on Lionel's new articulated flatcar pairs or the paired Maxi-Stack cars.

Lionel railroading has now been brought into the modern intermodal age, opening up new operating vistas for Lionel railroaders. This is all to the good, since variety sustains interest in a hobby. Lionel's little road vehicles have been one of the biggest hits of the modern era, and there is no reason to suppose that interest in these trucks will abate anytime soon.

GENERAL DISCUSSION

Except for the first three entries below and as noted, all of Lionel's tractor-trailer combinations share the following characteristics:

1. The tractors are die-cast with black plastic undercarriages and plastic trim pieces; they have black rubber tires. The hood opens to reveal a chromed engine. The base of the tractor contains an embossed circle-L logo and "LIONEL / Made In Macao". (This is an important detail in regard to the 12842 Dunkin' Donuts tractors and trailers.)

Fundimensions began offering tractor and trailer units in 1977 and 1978 with the Workin' On The Railroad sets. Three unnumbered models were available: Ryder Rental (top) and Santa Fe and Penn Central (second). Nothing came of this trend until after Lionel Trains Inc. started producing the line and brought out the 12725 Lionel in 1988 and the 12739 Lionel Gas Company in 1989 (third). The following year LTI expanded the line with the 12777 Chevron and 12778 Conrail (bottom).

Exc   Mint

2. There are several types of plastic trailer units, box, tank, and flat; all are mounted upon a die-cast frame with a plastic wheel undercarriage and trim pieces and a plastic swing-down set of support wheels. The plastic trailers are stamped "C. LIONEL TRAINS, INC.", and the frames are embossed with the same lettering as the tractors. The box trailers snap off the frames by pulling back a sliding plastic lock inside them; a no. 71-2725-251 instruction sheet is provided for assistance. The flatbed and tank trailers cannot be separated from their frames, however.

[NO NUMBERS] TRACTORS AND FLATBED TRAILERS, 1977–78

All-plastic tractor and trailer units were provided with the Workin' On The Railroad sets available in 1977 and 1978; they were never offered for separate sale. There were two varieties of the tractor units: The Ryder and Penn Central tractors were square-cab units, and the Santa Fe was a conventional cab-with-hood unit. The trailers were also of two types: The Ryder and Penn Central units came with an unlettered yellow open flatbed trailer with simulated stakes and upright supports, and the Santa Fe came with a dark blue unlettered plain flatbed trailer.

(A) Santa Fe; red cab-and-hood tractor with white Santa Fe cross logo.

5   10

(B) Penn Central; bright green square-cab tractor with white Penn Central logo.

5   10

(C) Ryder Rental; bright yellow square-cab tractor with red, black, and white Ryder logo.

5   10

[NO NUMBERS] TRACTOR AND TRAILER WITH STAKES, 1992–97

Red tractor, no other markings; came with red flatbed trailer with gray side stakes and red crate load; included in no. 11727 Coastal Limited set and several others.

CP

12725 LIONEL TRACTOR AND TRAILER, 1988–89

Bright orange tractor with blue stripe and lettering, chrome bumper, grill, and exhaust stack, bright orange trailer with white outline lettering "LIONEL" and Lionel logo.

20   30

Exc   Mint

12739 LIONEL GAS COMPANY TRACTOR AND TANKER 1989

Blue tractor with orange markings, chrome bumper, grill, and exhaust stack, gray tank trailer with white lettering and chrome trim.

15   20

12765 DIE-CAST AUTOMOBILE ASSORTMENT, 1990

Six die-cast metal automobiles (catalog states there were to be three Buicks and three Corvettes). This auto assortment was to have been similar to the cars provided with the 16208 Pennsylvania Railroad auto carrier of 1989; however, these cars were done in HO scale, and the auto carrier car was about to undergo a radical redesign. Therefore, these cars were never made.

Not manufactured

12777 CHEVRON TRACTOR AND TANKER, 1990–91

Red tractor with chrome trim, white tank trailer with Chevron logo, chrome trim, and red and black stripes at top of tank.

10   15

12778 CONRAIL TRACTOR AND TRAILER, 1990

Blue tractor with chrome trim and white lettering, white trailer with blue lettering and Conrail logo.

15   20

12779 LIONELVILLE GRAIN COMPANY TRACTOR AND GRAIN TRAILER, 1990

White tractor with chrome trim, gray striping and Lionel logo, dark gray trailer with red lettering and black simulated roping to hold down detachable light yellow trailer top.

10   15

12783 MONON CORPORATION TRACTOR AND TRAILER 1991

Black tractor with white lettering and chrome trim, white trailer with purple and black Monon lettering and gold eagle logo.

15   20

12784 THREE INTERMODAL CONTAINERS, 1991

Three trailer bodies, each separately numbered as follows: 12787 silver trailer, "THE FAMILY LINES

A new style of trailer was introduced in 1990 with the 12779 Lionelville Grain Company (right). It was joined a year later by the 12785 L. T. I. Gravel Company (left) and the 12783 Monon Corporation (center).

Exc Mint

SYSTEM" in blue with red, white, and blue logo; 12788 silver trailer, "UNION PACIFIC" in red with blue stripe and lettering and Union Pacific shield logo; 12789 white trailer, "BOSTON & MAINE" in black with light and dark blue striping. These containers are designed for use with the Lionel intermodal cranes, but they can also be snapped onto the wheel structure of any current Lionel trailer for road use. Although numbered separately, all three are sold as one package.

15 20

12785 L. T. I. GRAVEL COMPANY TRACTOR AND TRAILER, 1991

Silver tractor with chrome trim, blue striping and lettering, dark blue grain trailer with yellow lettering, white simulated roping to hold down detachable light gray roof.

10 15

12786 LIONELVILLE STEEL COMPANY TRACTOR AND TRAILER, 1991

Red tractor with white stripe and lettering, red flat trailer with white fencing and silver simulated steel rod loads.

10 15

Exc Mint

12794 LIONEL LINES TRACTOR UNIT, 1991

Orange tractor with chrome trim, dark blue stripe and lettering; appears to be identical to tractor supplied with 12725 tractor and trailer.

10 15

12805 THREE INTERMODAL CONTAINERS, 1992

Three trailer-containers, each separately numbered as follows: 11730 dark green container with large white "EVERGREEN" lettering; 11731 white container with blue and white star burst emblem and black "MAERSK" lettering; 11732 white container with red American President thunderbird emblem and red stripe at front of container. These containers were not sold separately.

10 15

12806 LIONEL LUMBER COMPANY TRACTOR AND TRAILER, 1992

Dark green tractor with silver stripe and lettering, gray flatbed trailer with stakes (identical to those on Standard O flatcars) and black "LIONELVILLE LUMBER, INC." lettering, set of three large varnished dowels made up as logs.

10 15

Exc	Mint

12807 LITTLE CAESARS TRACTOR AND TRAILER, 1992

White tractor with orange and black Little Caesars emblem; white trailer with black "Little Caesars Pizza! Pizza!" and orange and black emblem, orange stripe at bottom edge with white lettering.

10   15

12808 MOBIL TRACTOR AND TANKER, 1992

Light tan tractor with black lettering, gray tanker with chrome top ports and white undercarriage, blue and red "MOBIL" lettering and red and white flying horse logo. Now difficult to find; Mobil Oil has since issued its own tractor and tanker.

20   30

12810 AMERICAN FLYER TRACTOR AND TRAILER, 1992

Dark blue tractor with yellow lettering, dark blue trailer with wide yellow stripe and blue and yellow "AMERICAN FLYER" steam train logo and lettering.

15   20

Exc	Mint

12811 ALKA-SELTZER TRACTOR AND TRAILER, 1992

White tractor with red and black "MILES" logo, white trailer with green, black, red, and white "ALKA-SELTZER" packets on black background.

10   15

12819 INLAND STEEL TRACTOR AND FLATBED TRAILER, 1992

Red tractor with white stripe and lettering, white flatbed trailer with red "INLAND STEEL" lettering and load of five plastic simulated steel girders.

10   15

12826 THREE INTERMODAL CONTAINERS, 1993

Three trailer-containers, each separately numbered as follows: 12827 white container with dark blue "CSX" logo and lettering; 12828 silver container with yellow and black logo and black and white New York Central logo; 12829 dark green container with wide orange stripe edged by yellow stripes, yellow "GREAT NORTHERN" lettering, and red and white

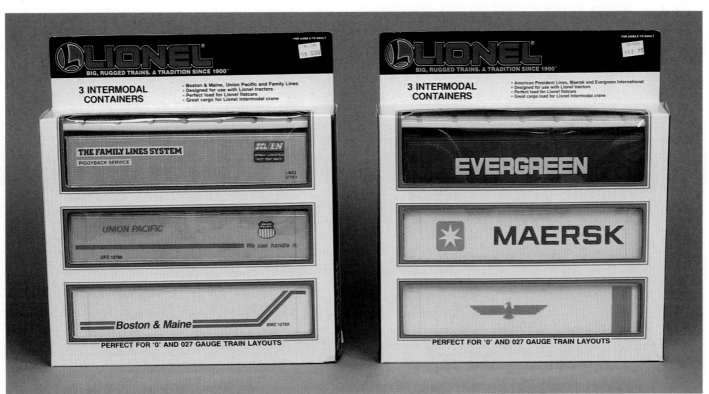

Yet another innovation appeared in 1991, when LTI introduced sets of intermodal containers for use with its intermodal cranes. The 12784 three-pack (left) was cataloged in 1991, and the 12805 three-pack (right) was cataloged the next year.

Tractors with flatbed trailers were the next notable design. The 12786 Lionelville Steel Company (left) and the 12806 Lionel Lumber Company (right) heralded the new style. A popular tractor and trailer combination for 1992 was the 12807 Little Caesars (center).

Also in 1992, LTI increased its roster of tractor and trailer combinations with the 12810 American Flyer (left), 12808 Mobil (center), and 12811 Alka-Seltzer (right).

Moving full speed ahead with its line of tractor and trailer rigs, LTI cataloged the 12833 RoadRailer (left) and 12836 Santa Fe Quantum (center) in 1993 and the 12819 Inland Steel (right) the previous year.

	Exc	Mint

goat herald. These containers were not sold separately.

	10	15

12833 ROADRAILER TRACTOR AND TRAILER, 1993

Red tractor with white stripe and lettering, white trailer with red and black "ROADRAILER" logo and black lettering.

	10	15

12836 SANTA FE QUANTUM TRACTOR AND TRAILER, 1993

Black tractor with red striping and circle-L logo, white trailer with blue, black, and yellow "QUANTUM" logo and black lettering with blue number.

	10	15

12837 HUMBLE TRACTOR AND TANKER, 1993

Silver tractor with red striping and Humble oval logo, gray tank with chrome top ports, white ladder, chrome side pipes, red oval "HUMBLE" logo, and blue rectangle "PETROLEUM PRODUCTS".

	10	15

	Exc	Mint

12842 DUNKIN' DONUTS TRACTOR AND TRAILER, 1992

White tractor with orange and purple Dunkin' Donuts logo, white trailer with variety of doughnuts along side with counter attendant and "DUNKIN' DONUTS: IT'S WORTH THE TRIP" towards rear. This Lionel tractor and trailer unit is of interest because the Dunkin' Donuts firm decided to commission its own tractor-trailer units for special promotion, and the first of these that appeared in late 1993 are almost identical to Lionel's. The latter came in typical Type VI packaging, but the Dunkin' Donuts version has its own packaging, though its configuration is identical to Lionel's.

A careful examination of the two units will enable collectors and operators to tell them apart. The country of origin for Lionel's unit is Macao; for the Dunkin' Donuts unit it is China. The instruction sheets packed into each trailer are interesting. Lionel's has the Lionel identification and part number, while the Dunkin' Donuts sheet has that company's logo. However, the drawings and wording on the sheets are absolutely identical! The only difference is that on the Lionel sheet the drawings are labeled Figures 1, 2, and 3, while on the Dunkin' Donuts sheet the figures are A, B, and C.

The tractor has its own distinctions as well. Lionel's is lettered on the bottom; this lettering is absent from the Dunkin' Donuts version (as well as on

After LTI produced the 12842 Dunkin' Donuts tractor and trailer (left) in 1992, the advertiser was so pleased that it went ahead and commissioned its own rigs in unique packaging (right) as part of a special promotion for 1993.

Exc Mint

the trailer frame and container). The riveting on the Dunkin' Donuts is larger than that on the Lionel, and so is the door handle on the cab. The rubber tires on the Lionel version carry Lionel lettering, as can be seen upon a close examination; the Dunkin' Donuts version does not have any lettering. On the chrome radiator grill, the middle vertical dividing line on the Lionel version is shorter than the other two; on the Dunkin' Donuts, these lines are of equal length. The rivets on the undercarriage of the Dunkin' Donuts version are cruder than those on the Lionel tractor. Finally, the black plastic of the undercarriage of the Lionel version is shiny, while that of the Dunkin' Donuts tractor is dull—the same difference found between original and reproduction automobiles for the postwar 6414 Auto Loader.

On the trailer, one obvious difference is that the Lionel version has the wording "IT'S WORTH THE TRIP"; this slogan is missing from the Dunkin' Donuts trailer. In addition, the doughnuts portrayed on the Dunkin' Donuts trailer are of the same general pattern as those on the Lionel trailer, but they are much larger. The large "DUNKIN' DONUTS" lettering on the trailer is in front of the counter attendant on the Lionel version, but behind him on the Dunkin' Donuts. The rear of the Lionel trailer is plain, but there is a "1994" plate on the Dunkin' Donuts version. Finally, the stub attaching the trailer frame to the tractor is longer on the Lionel version than it is on the Dunkin' Donuts.

These differences should enable collectors and operators to distinguish the Lionel version from its Dunkin' Donuts successor. This point is somewhat

Exc Mint

important because the late-1992 Lionel tractor-trailer is scarcer than the Dunkin' Donuts units. Later Dunkin' Donuts rigs have different graphics on their trailers; as a result, there is no identification problem with them.

35   45

12852 EXTRA TRAILER FRAME, 1994–97

Die-cast trailer frame packaged in plastic bag. These frames are meant to equip box trailers sold in intermodal container assortments with their own frames for placement atop flatcars.

CP

12854 U. S. NAVY ROCKET FUEL TRACTOR AND TANKER, 1994–95

Gray tractor with black lettering; white tanker trailer with chromed top ports and pipes, gray tank with black "UNITED STATES NAVY ROCKET FUEL". This tractor-tanker is part of the no. 11745 U. S. Navy Train Set and was not offered for separate sale.

25   30

12855 THREE INTERMODAL CONTAINERS, 1994–95

Three trailer-containers, each separately numbered as follows: 12856 silver container with red "CP RAIL" lettering and black, red, and white Pac-Man logo; 12857 silver container with red lettering and

Recent additions to the line of tractor and trailer combinations include the 12864 Little Caesars (left), 12865 Wisk (center), and 12837 Humble (right).

	Exc	Mint

Frisco logo; 12858 silver container with green Vermont Railway logo and white lettering. These containers were not sold separately.

15 20

12860 LIONEL VISITOR'S CENTER TRACTOR AND TRAILER, 1994

Bright blue tractor with silver striping and circle-L logo; silver trailer with large blue wing stripe edged in black containing red "VISITOR'S CENTER" and circle-L logo, black script lettering "THE MAGIC LIVES ON".

25 30

12861 LIONEL LEASING CORPORATION TRACTOR UNIT, 1994

Dark maroon tractor with silver "LIONEL LEASING CORP." lettering.

7 10

12864 LITTLE CAESARS TRACTOR AND TRAILER, 1994

White tractor with black Little Caesars circular emblem; white trailer with large Little Caesars figure eating pizza with two pizzas impaled on spear; blue and orange stripes run across trailer; orange, black, and white Little Caesars emblem followed by black

	Exc	Mint

lettering "LITTLE CAESARS" above orange and blue lines and black-outlined orange "PIZZA! PIZZA!" below. Compare with 12807.

10 15

12865 WISK TRACTOR AND TRAILER, 1994

Bright royal blue tractor with white "LEVER"; bright royal blue trailer with white "DOUBLE POWER" and orange-red and yellow "WISK"; plastic bottle of Wisk with yellow cap.

10 15

12869 MARATHON OIL TRACTOR AND TANKER, 1994

Bright blue tractor with white "MARATHON OIL COMPANY", gray tank trailer with chrome upper ports and pipes, red, white, and blue Marathon logo and blue and red striping, white lettering "AN AMERICAN COMPANY SERVING AMERICA", red, white, and black warning diamond.

10 15

12875 LIONEL RAILROADER CLUB TRACTOR AND TRAILER, 1994

Red tractor with white "LIONEL LINES"; white trailer with red front section and longitudinal striping,

These tractor and trailer combinations show how well these models can promote Lionel and various collector clubs The 12860 (left) came out in 1994, not long after the Lionel Visitor's Center opened. The 52021 Weyerhaeuser (center) was issued to mark the Toy Train Operating Society's national convention in 1993. The 12875 Lionel Railroader Club (right) was introduced in 1994 as a premium to those people who became members.

	Exc	Mint

black and white "RRC", red and black lettering "DELIVERING THE LIONEL MAGIC TO YOU!"

	25	**35**

12881 CHRYSLER MOPAR TRACTOR AND TRAILER, 1994

White tractor with red, black, and blue Mopar logo; white trailer with Mopar logos. Part of uncataloged Mopar promotional set.

	30	**40**

12891 LIONEL LINES REFRIGERATOR LINES TRACTOR AND TRAILER, 1995

Black tractor with white "LIONEL LINES"; orange trailer with silver roof and gray refrigeration unit piece added to front; black and white penguin decor, black "LIONEL REFRIGERATOR LINES" with blue frost trim, red and white thermometer with black "COLDER THAN ICE!"

	10	**15**

12907 THREE INTERMODAL CONTAINERS, 1995

Three trailer-containers, each separately numbered as follows: 12908 white container with red "NP" emblem and red, black, and white Northern Pacific circular monad logo; 12909 silver container with red and black "CP RAIL INTERMODAL FREIGHT SYSTEMS" logo; 12910 silver container with red "WESTERN PACIFIC" lettering in yellow rectangle, second yellow rectangle with "SERVICE" trailer logo and black "Rail / Road" lettering. These containers were not sold separately.

CP

12932 LAIMBEER PACKAGING TRACTOR AND TRAILER, 1996–97

White tractor unit with chrome trim; white trailer unit with red, white, and blue "LAIMBEER PACKAGING" logo on sides. This company, owned by former NBA star Bill Laimbeer, supplies Lionel with its packaging cartons. This tractor-trailer unit is the first to be packaged in a Type VII Lionel box.

CP

12935 ZENITH TRACTOR AND TRAILER, 1996

White tractor with red Zenith logo, white trailer with red Zenith "lightning" logo and black "The Quality Goes In Before the Name Goes On". The number GP5094-1295 is present on the box end flap, in addition

Front: The striking 12869 Marathon Oil Tractor and Tanker was cataloged in 1994. Rear: The 12891 Lionel Lines Refrigerator Lines made its first appearance the following year.

	Exc	Mint

to the 12935 number. This unit reportedly was included in a promotional set made for Zenith by Lionel.

                                             —   45

16357 LOUISVILLE & NASHVILLE TRACTOR UNIT, 1992

Silver tractor with red stripe and lettering; matches silver trailer with red "L & N" logo and lettering. Trailer came with 16357 Louisville & Nashville flatcar in no. 11729 L & N Express set.

                                        7   10

16383 LIONEL LINES TRACTOR UNIT, 1993

Blue tractor with white striping and "LIONEL LINES"; matches white trailer with blue and gray "CONRAIL MERCURY" logos. Trailer came with 16383 Conrail flatcar in no. 11740 Conrail Consolidated set.

                                        7   10

16398 CHESAPEAKE & OHIO TRACTOR UNIT, 1994

Dark blue tractor with yellow Chesapeake & Ohio logo; matches silver trailer with white striping and lettering "PIGGYBACK SERVICE" and yellow and blue circular "C & O" logo. Trailer came with 16398 Chesapeake & Ohio flatcar in no. 11743 C & O Freight set.

                                        7   10

17894 TTOS SOUTHERN PACIFIC TRACTOR, 1991

White tractor; white trailer with orange "TTOS TRANSPORTATION" lettering.

                                   20   25

17896 LCCA LANCASTER LINES TRACTOR UNIT, 1991

White tractor with red or blue lettering. The unit with red lettering was available at only the Lionel Collectors Club of America national convention; the one with blue lettering was available before and after the convention by mail order.

(A) Red LCCA lettering.

                                   25   30

(B) Blue LCCA lettering.

                                   15   20

The Lionel Collectors Club of America has used several special tractor and trailer combinations to promote itself. These unique items include the 52025 Madison Hardware Company (front) in 1993 and the 52055 Sovex (rear) in 1994.

	Exc	Mint

52021 TTOS WEYERHAEUSER TRACTOR AND TRAILER, 1993

White tractor with bright green exhaust stacks and steps, green Weyerhaeuser logo and lettering on door; white flatbed trailer with bright green perimeter stakes and supports, green "T.T.O.S. PORTLAND, OREGON 1993" and "BUILT BY LIONEL 8-93". This tractor-trailer often accompanied a matching Standard O boxcar produced for the same event.

25   30

52025 LCCA MADISON HARDWARE COMPANY TRACTOR AND TRAILER, 1993

Bright blue tractor with triangular orange stripe across hood and orange "MADISON HARDWARE"; dark gray and orange trailer with black "MADISON HARD-WARE CO. / LIONEL ELECTRIC TRAINS / SPECIAL SHIPMENT" and black circular Lionel Service logo and lettering, white "BLT 12-93 / LIONEL".

25   35

	Exc	Mint

52028 TTOS SET OF THREE FORD AUTOMOBILES, 1994

Three die-cast black Ford automobiles with white oval "FORD" script logo and white "TTOS DEARBORN MICH. 8-94"; came in unmarked white box.

25   35

52033 TTOS WOLVERINE DIVISION TRACTOR AND TRAILER, 1995

Cream-colored tractor with blue lettering and circle-L Lionel logo, cream and orange trailer with blue, orange, and white rectangular "Lionel Electric Trains" logo. The 52033 came in a box with a 52040 Grand Trunk flatcar in orange with TTOS markings. According to the built dates, the flatcar was made the year before the tractor-trailer. Value given is for the tractor and trailer; add $30 for flatcar and outer carton.

—   35

To mark its national convention and the tour that members received of Carail, the Toy Train Operating Society offered the 52069 Carail Tractor and Trailer and the companion 52053 boxcar.

	Exc	Mint

52055 LCCA SOVEX TRACTOR AND TRAILER, 1994

Dark brown tractor with gold Sovex lettering; white trailer with brown, red, and yellow "GOOD SHEPHERD" logo, three multicolored packages of Good Shepherd cereal products in rectangle.

25   35

52056 LCCA SOUTHERN TRACTOR AND TRAILER, 1994

Green tractor with circular white "SR" logo; silver trailer with green "SOUTHERN RAILWAY SYSTEM" in white rectangle, green "SOUZ 206502" letters and numbers at upper right.

25   35

	Exc	Mint

52069 TTOS CARAIL TRACTOR AND TRAILER, 1994

White tractor; white trailer with red, white, and blue circle-L Lionel emblem and light blue Carail script logo; came with white 52053 Carail flatcar with dark blue "T. T. O. S. National Convention / Dearborn, Michigan / August 3 through 7, 1994".

25   35

52091 LENNOX TRACTOR AND TRAILER, 1995

White tractor with black Lennox address and chrome trim; white trailer with large black, yellow, and red human figure and logo and yellow lettering.

35

10
MAINTENANCE AND SMALL PARTS

"Have you practiced your music?" [Harry Truman] wrote to [his daughter] Margaret from Camp Ripley, Minnesota another summer. He had splurged and for Christmas bought her a baby grand piano, a Steinway, a surprise she did not appreciate. She had dreamed of an electric train.
— David McCullough, *Truman*

INTRODUCTION

One of the most remarkable and, to many, endearing elements about Lionel trains is that they are so systematic in nature. A set is never a self-contained toy; it interacts with a large number of other train-related elements. That is why model railroaders can create such totally individual empires. When everything works the way it should, it is an operator's triumph. When it doesn't work out quite so well, that's where maintenance items come into the picture. Basic maintenance by means of the right instruction books, parts, and "little" items can keep a railroad operating as it should. Besides, that is where the educational elements of Lionel trains can be outstanding.

The earliest Lionel trains were memorable for many reasons, but one usually neglected topic of conversation is the well-designed and clear instruction sheets the firm made for its sets and individual pieces. Collectors of Lionel paper have known for many years that no toy of any kind ever had such efficient operating and maintenance instructions written for it. One of the biggest factors in Lionel's success over all of its production phases has been the clear instructions given to its purchasers concerning how to run a train and maintain it properly.

To be sure, sometimes in the old days the instructions were a little ghastly by our safety-conscious standards. One very early hookup (before transformers) advised using a lightbulb as a resistor with a regular electric power outlet. If the wires ever got crossed, there would be live 120-volt current in the tracks! Instruction sheets of the 1920s advised train operators to "clean the tracks regularly with a little gasoline." Not exactly the stuff of safety for the kiddies!

This phase of instructions soon passed as the trains were made totally safe by means of the low-voltage transformer. Lionel eliminated the track-cleaning problem with a safe cleaning formula. In the postwar years instruction sheets became truly comprehensive, and Lionel provided an outstanding service manual for its retail outlets. Many operators possess excellent reproductions of these documents today.

Lionel also published magazines and handbooks for consumers with many building and maintenance tips. The importance of these documents cannot be understated as a factor in the success of Lionel trains. No other toy was so thoroughly documented, explained, and demonstrated by its literature.

In the postwar years, Lionel also marketed something else to help operators: spare parts available to the consumer. This wasn't just a matter of smoke pellets or track cleaning fluid, either. Replacement coal, barrels, logs, and many other types of small parts were made available in case of breakage or loss; these parts are now quite valuable among collectors. Many operators remember the excellent 927 Maintenance Kit, sold for a long time in the postwar era. It had track cleaner, smoke pellets, cleaning cloths, emery boards, small brushes, oil, grease, and even a wood tamper to shove smoke pellets down the smokestacks of the great steam engines of the age.

In the modern era, Fundimensions and Lionel Trains Inc. have not been quite so comprehensive in offering spare parts and maintenance items for consumers, but that has begun to change in recent years. From the beginning, Fundimensions marketed a maintenance kit in shrink-wrap that used leftover postwar oilers, smoke fluid, grease, and an eraser-type track cleaner. It wasn't as comprehensive as the old 927 maintenance kits, but it provided what was needed. For a time, even leftover bottles of postwar smoke pellets were marketed for older locomotives; the bottles were sold in Type I shrink-wrap packaging and are difficult to find today. One of the stranger offerings of the early modern era was the 2980 magnetic conversion coupler kit, which originally was marketed in the late 1940s as the 480-32. It came in a little white envelope and represented one more effort on the part of Fundimensions to market leftover material. But what could these kits be used for? The coupler was designed to be crimped over the axles of the wheel sets. That was fine with postwar wheel sets because they did not rotate. But the new fast-angle wheel sets featured fixed axles that did rotate. And what coupler was being replaced? The kit did come in handy for postwar cars with broken couplers, but it was a strange part to market.

During LTI's tenure, packages of coal, logs, barrels, and other decorative parts began to be sold, and these came in handy for those little extra touches around a layout. Cable reels, crate loads, and coil covers for gondolas soon followed; separately sold ore loads were marketed for the little ore cars marketed by LTI in the late 1980s.

It has been wise for Lionel to recognize the large potential aftermarket audience for replacement and extra parts. At the rate these are being released, it will not be long before they surpass the offerings from the postwar years. It is one more step in making Lionel the truly complete marketer of toy trains.

2909 SMOKE FLUID, 1970–95

Early versions in Type I shrink-wrap; later ones sold without extra packaging; clear plastic bottles have blue markings until 1988, when formula was changed and bottles were given red Lionel markings. Smoke fluid in little plastic bottles is one of the few items to have been offered throughout the modern era; after all, it is a necessity for steam locomotives. The early smoke fluid never worked well, and in the 1980s competing brands of liquid smoke appeared,

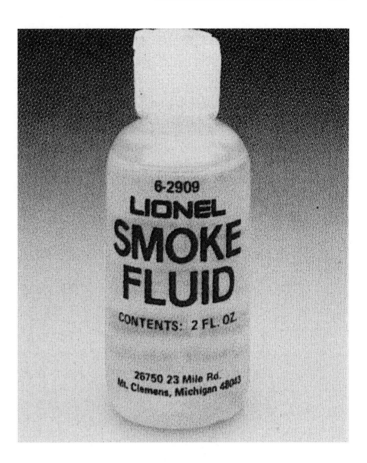

The 2909 Smoke Fluid has been a standard part of the Lionel line since 1970.

	Exc	Mint

such as Supersmoke, which worked much better than Lionel's material. Around 1988, the formula for Lionel's smoke fluid was changed, and the new formula works much better. Even so, the Seuthe-type smoke units in certain accessories and rolling stock seem to work better with thinner formulas such as the one made by LGB for its large scale trains. A word of warning here for operators who have young children: The Lionel smoke fluid, as well as smoke fluids made by LGB and others, is a petroleum distillate and therefore toxic when swallowed. Supersmoke, by Bart's Pneumatics, claims to be nontoxic. Other nontoxic formulas may be available; shop around! **Cross-reference:** PW 909.

CP

2911 SMOKE PELLETS, 1970–72

Postwar bottles of 50 pellets with white, orange, and blue label marked "SP LIONEL SMOKE PELLETS"; Type I shrink-wrap or pillbox. Many collectors and operators do not realize that Fundimensions did market the obsolete SP Smoke Pellets during the first

Exc Mint

years of its operations. Those bottles were leftover production shrink-wrapped into Type I packaging. This was just one more example of Fundimensions' ability to make the most of leftover materials; after all, any proceeds would be "found money" to help finance new types of production. The only way to identify the bottles of SP Pellets as Fundimensions production is to find them in the original shrink-wrap packaging, which is exceedingly difficult. This packaging has been authenticated by photographs. **Cross-reference:** PW SP.

20   25

2927 MAINTENANCE KIT, 1970–71 and 1977–97

Consists of lubricant, oiler, track cleaning fluid, and rubber eraser-type track cleaner, all mounted on a piece of cardboard and shrink-wrapped. The marketing history of this accessory has been a little unusual.

Exc Mint

Leftover materials were packaged in Type I shrink-wrap packaging and sold that way for the first two years of the Fundimensions regime. Then it apparently disappeared as a kit, although many of the components were available separately. (If anyone has seen a kit in Type II packaging, we would like verification.) In 1977, the kit reappeared, this time in Type III packaging, and it was available this way until the last year of Fundimensions in 1986. The kit was then sold by LTI with the same materials but slightly altered markings and Type VI packaging, which has been the case up to the present. Type I examples are difficult to find in their original shrink-wrap. **Cross-references:** PW 927, 928.

(A) Type I packaging (same scheme as Type I box), lubricant, oiler, track-cleaning fluid, and eraser-type track cleaner; leftover postwar production with Hillside, New Jersey, factory address.

15   20

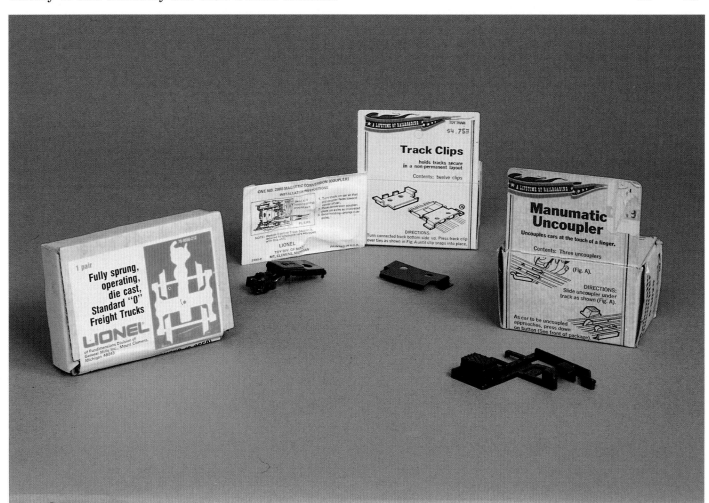

Among the items Model Products Corp. offered to maintain and upgrade Lionel trains were (left to right): 9550 Die-Cast Standard "O" Trucks, and 2980 Magnetic Conversion Coupler Kit; the 2901 Track Clips and 5025 Manumatic Uncoupler were used with track.

	Exc	Mint

(B) Type III packaging, Fundimensions-produced materials.

| | 7 | 10 |

(C) Type VI shrink-wrap packaging, LTI-produced materials.

| | **CP** |

2980 MAGNETIC CONVERSION COUPLER KIT, 1971 and 1979–80

Kit for replacing other types of couplers with magnetic operating couplers; consists of plate assembly and either a Delrin plastic coupler with integrally molded leaf spring mounted with a chrome rivet or a die-cast knuckle coupler, knuckle spring, and chrome rivet. It was strange that Fundimensions placed this kit on the market in 1971 because it could work only with postwar cars that had broken coupler assemblies. Even stranger, the firm brought out a version in 1979 with a different assembly for a different purpose. The 1979 kit had a plastic coupler instead of the postwar unit, and it was probably meant to replace the nonoperating couplers found on some low-end rolling stock of the time. The later version came with a separate instruction sheet; the 1971 one had its instructions printed in blue right on the small white envelope. The illustration on this envelope came from the postwar service manual. We would like comments on the 1979–80 version. **Cross-reference:** PW 480-32.

(A) 1971, small white parts envelope with blue instructions printed directly thereupon; leftover postwar die-cast coupler with metal plate enclosed.

| | 7 | 10 |

(B) 1979–80, envelope with separate instruction sheet, plastic truck and coupler to be mounted with chrome rivet.

| | 5 | 7 |

8190 DIESEL HORN KIT, 1981

Electronic package that can be adapted to locomotives and rolling stock, operated by whistle button on older transformer; Type V box includes circuit board, speaker, two double-sided adhesive pads, and instructions. Roller pickup assembly must be purchased separately if needed; unit can be installed with existing roller pickups. Kit was an attempt to give operators an opportunity to install diesel horns in the many locomotives of the 1970s that did not have them. The first Fundimensions attempt at a diesel horn came in 1973 and, like this version, it was electronic. But that horn could not be operated efficiently with older transform-

ers because after it was triggered by the pickup voltage of the whistle/horn levers, it could not be sustained by the holding voltage position. (Postwar whistles and horns depended upon a strong shot of DC to activate, but holding the switch at its first stage would also cause a sharp rattling sound from the E-unit reversing switch. A lesser holding voltage at the switch's second position solved that problem for postwar units.) The early horn had a diode-activated switch wired into the main circuit (Fundimensions' early steam whistles worked the same way). However, these diodes often stuck in the closed position, which caused them to burn out. These diesel horns were discontinued after less than a year; as a result, dummy diesel locomotives with this horn are difficult to find and highly prized. A new diesel horn was introduced in the 8157 Santa Fe Train Master, and it solved the pickup voltage problem. This kit was supposed to retrofit earlier locomotives. Values for unused unit only.

| | 35 | 45 |

9550 PAIR OF DIE-CAST STANDARD "O" TRUCKS, 1973–74

Two Standard O trucks in 3" x 5" x 1" white cardboard container with red and white label (part no. 70-9550-212); label has a white silhouette of truck on red background and black "FULLY SPRUNG / OPERATING / DIE CAST / STANDARD 'O' / FREIGHT TRUCKS". Many collectors and operators are not even aware that Fundimensions marketed extra sets of the excellent Standard O trucks when it introduced the Standard O cars late in 1973. They were, of course, designed to retrofit other varieties of Lionel rolling stock. The trucks, which came in a small white cardboard box with screw fasteners and an instruction sheet, are difficult to find. **Cross-reference:** ME 12843.

| | 25 | 35 |

12732 COAL BAG, 1988–97

Four ounces of plastic coal pieces packed in white sack with red lettering and logo and string tie. Aftermarket manufacturers have sold replicas of Lionel 206 Coal in little cloth bags for many years. LTI finally reinstituted the sale of its own simulated coal with this little cloth bag, which duplicates the packaging of the postwar product. It is doubtful Lionel's plastic coal differs from anyone else's. **Cross-references:** PW 206, 207.

| | **CP** |

12740 LOG PACKAGE, 1988–97

Set of three wood logs with bark to retrofit log dump cars or supply flatcar loads; comes in plastic bag.

Lionel Trains Inc. offered a variety of items to use with its accessories and rolling stock. These included the 12732 Coal Bag, 12745 Barrel Pack, and 12795 Cable Reels.

Exc   Mint

This accessory is simplicity itself: three sections of twigs cut into miniature logs for a logging empire or flatcars. At the risk of being irreverent, it is just as easy to get the same accessory by strolling outside with a pair of tree lopper shears. It is also just as realistic, since these are real wood!

CP

12745 BARREL PACK, 1989–97

Six small dark brown varnished wood barrels packaged in a plastic bag. Unlike the plain barrels of the postwar era, these barrels are highly varnished. Operators of the barrel car or ramp (not reissued to

Exc   Mint

date) should be aware that varnished barrels often are too "slippery" to be vibrated up the ramps of these accessories. The drum-shaped barrels often packed with 6462 gondolas have not been reissued, but are plentiful on the toy train market. **Cross-reference: PW 362-78.**

CP

12753 ORE LOAD, 1989–97

Red-brown simulated ore load in form of plastic shell that fits into Lionel ore cars; sold in pairs in plastic bag. LTI marketed these loads after noticing that sales of similar items were brisk on the toy train

Exc Mint

aftermarket. Many operators made up huge unit trains of LTI's ore cars, so selling these custom-fit loads made great sense.

CP

12795 TWO CABLE REELS, 1991–97

Pair of light gray cable reels with black "LIONEL"; reels are like those that came with the 6561 Cable Reel Car and various postwar and modern-era cars and accessories. They do not have the wound metal wire found on examples of the 6561; instead, they are made like the late postwar examples that came with gondolas and flatcars. **Cross-reference:** PW 40-50.

CP

12800 SCALE HUDSON REPLACEMENT PILOT TRUCK, 1991

Four-wheel pilot truck somewhat resembling the one found on postwar Hudson locomotives, such as the 646 and 665. Smaller wheels than those on the scale truck allow operation on modern tubular track. Scale pilot truck can be remounted for display. When LTI's replica of the prewar 700E Scale Hudson was issued (catalog number 18005 in 1990), operators found to their dismay that the large pilot wheels would derail going over modern-era switches and crossovers. (The prewar Hudson was designed to run on Lionel's scale flat-rail track.) To remedy this problem, LTI offered a replacement pilot truck for operation that would allow the locomotive to run on tubular track. Its wheels were considerably smaller than the scale wheels of the model as issued.

15   20

12838 CRATE LOAD, 1993–97

Assortment of plastic truck and carloads ("LCL" cargo) for multiple use; molded in one unpainted color (catalog shows red); sold in plastic bags. This accessory is simplicity itself: 27-piece assortment of unpainted crates, pipes, rods, and other loads suitable for use on trucks and rolling stock.

CP

12843 PAIR OF DIE-CAST SPRUNG TRUCKS, 1993–97

Two sets of die-cast sprung Standard O trucks with mounting screws and rivets; Type VI packaging. The emergence of LTI's fine Standard O freight cars made the release of spare sprung trucks inevitable and desirable to convert older rolling stock with plastic

The 12838 Crate Load was cataloged from 1993 to 1995 to provide an array of items to be hauled on LTI's freight cars and tractor-trailer combinations.

Exc   Mint

trucks. These are the excellent Standard O trucks first issued in late 1973. There may be detail differences between these trucks and those first issued in the little-known 9550 boxes of 1974. They come in Type VI packaging with rivets and mounting screws. **Cross-reference:** ME 9550.

CP

12844 O AND O27 GONDOLA COIL COVERS, 1993–97

Pair of light gray unlettered coil covers with pickup railings for use in regular-size O and O27 gondolas; sold in plastic bags. Since LTI's first issue of gondolas with coil covers, these covers have been popular, especially with specific road names. However, these unlettered coil covers add a dress-up look to any regular-size gondola. Pickup handles need assembly. **Cross-reference:** ME 12853.

CP

12853 STANDARD O COIL COVERS, 1994–97

Pair of light gray unlettered coil covers with pickup railings for use in Standard O gondolas; larger than

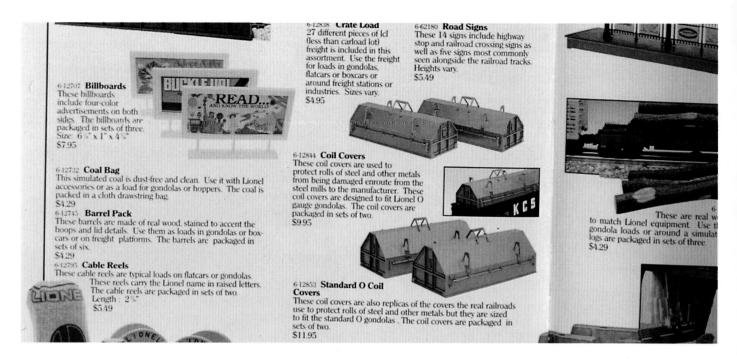

6-12707 Billboards
These billboards include four-color advertisements on both sides. The billboards are packaged in sets of three. Size: 6¼" x 1" x 4¼".
$7.95

6-12732 Coal Bag
This simulated coal is dust-free and clean. Use it with Lionel accessories or as a load for gondolas or hoppers. The coal is packed in a cloth drawstring bag.
$4.29

6-12745 Barrel Pack
These barrels are made of real wood, stained to accent the hoops and lid details. Use them as loads in gondolas or boxcars or on freight platforms. The barrels are packaged in sets of six.
$4.29

6-12795 Cable Reels
These cable reels are typical loads on flatcars or gondolas. These reels carry the Lionel name in raised letters. The cable reels are packaged in sets of two. Length: 2⅛".
$5.49

6-12838 Crate Load
27 different pieces of lcl (less than carload lot) freight is included in this assortment. Use the freight for loads in gondolas, flatcars or boxcars or around freight stations or industries. Sizes vary.
$4.95

6-12844 Coil Covers
These coil covers are used to protect rolls of steel and other metals from being damaged enroute from the steel mills to the manufacturer. These coil covers are designed to fit Lionel O gauge gondolas. The coil covers are packaged in sets of two.
$9.95

6-12853 Standard O Coil Covers
These coil covers are also replicas of the covers the real railroads use to protect rolls of steel and other metals but they are sized to fit the standard O gondolas. The coil covers are packaged in sets of two.
$11.95

6-62180 Road Signs
These 14 signs include highway stop and railroad crossing signs as well as five signs most commonly seen alongside the railroad tracks. Heights vary.
$5.49

These are real w to match Lionel equipment. Use th gondola loads or around a simulat logs are packaged in sets of three.
$4.29

Coil covers, essential parts on contemporary gondolas, were offered by LTI in two sizes. The 12844 set of two coil covers fit O and O27 gauge cars, and the 12853 set was designed for the larger, Standard O models.

	Exc	Mint

12844; sold in plastic bags. These coil covers are identical to those in the 12844, except they are designed to fit the larger Standard O gondolas, which some- times come with coil covers of their own. These covers are well-suited for the Fundimensions Standard O gondolas. **Cross-reference:** ME 12844. **CP**

11

TRACKS, TRANSFORMERS, AND RELATED PARTS

When a model system is planned, there are several primary considerations. Realism is always first, and to this end there must be no crowding. The trackage must look as if it belonged in its setting and not as if some geometric pattern were being followed, as happens so often with tinplate track.
—Edwin P. Alexander, *Model Railroads* (1940)
(Good thing Mr. Alexander never saw *my* layout. . . .)

INTRODUCTION

Lo, the lowly bumper. It's just one of many Lionel accessories that do not get the attention they deserve. The same goes for such items as the omnipresent CTC lockon or the O and O27 gauge track clips. Who pays attention to such things? Yet there are really interesting stories about even these humdrum members of the Lionel system.

Consider, for example, the reissue of the postwar 260 Bumper as the 2260 in the early years of Fundimensions. The heavy, die-cast version was not chosen for reissue until much later in the modern era. Instead, Fundimensions chose to reissue the bumper in its black plastic form; in the postwar years, this version of the 260 had been made to work with Super O track. Quite a few of these plastic 260 models had been left over, so Fundimensions reissued them in several formats — Type I boxes and Type II shrink-wrap packaging, for example. These examples retained the postwar white lettering on the bottom plate and were virtually indistinguishable from postwar models except for packaging. Then Fundimensions made more of these

bumpers, and this time they had no lettering on the bottom plate. The firm even made a nonilluminated version of the 2260 for its Pioneer Dockside Switcher set of 1972. For a time collectors and operators considered this version a regular 2260 from which the parts had been removed, but this is not the case.

One way to tell a 2260 from its 260 predecessor is to look at the mounting screws; in postwar versions they are slotted, while Fundimensions pieces have Phillips-head screws. Even that is insufficient, of course, since screws can be changed. Some postwar models have bright opaque red lens caps instead of translucent red ones, but these also can be changed.

There is also a great story about the O27 track clips that may be true or legendary, but it is certainly persistent. Supposedly, when Lionel bought out the Ives Corporation in 1931, one part of the agreement was that Lionel would keep the Ives name alive by placing it on one of its products. Lionel presumably did this by stamping the lowly O27 track clip with the Ives name for many years! This would seem a little vindictive for Joshua Lionel Cowen; the major reason he bought Ives was to secure the patent for Ives's three-position reversing switch, which was far superior to Lionel's old pendulum unit. Legend or reality, it's a pretty good story.

The lesson to be learned here is never to take *any* piece of Lionel's equipment for granted. Every item tells a story; even during the modern era collectors and Lionel historians must act as if they are toy train archaeologists deducing the past from a study of the artifacts. One of the most fascinating elements of these trains is, after

Among the new items developed by Model Products Corp. was the 2280 nonilluminated plastic bumper. It remained in the catalog from 1973 through 1984; three years later, Lionel Trains Inc. reissued it in Tuscan as the 12717 (shown here).

all, the idea that one can trace the history of a century-old American corporation by examining its products and relying on deductive reasoning. There's a little Sherlock Holmes in all Lionel enthusiasts!

2260 BUMPER, 1970–73

Black plastic body, four screws at corners, translucent red cap, (as opposed to bright solid red color), takes 14-volt bayonet-base bulb. Came in Type I box or Type II shrink-wrap packaging. Somewhat hard to find. See the Introduction for a full discussion of this accessory. It employs the same mold used for postwar 26 and 260 die-cast bumpers, but it has a black plastic body originally designed for Super O track. The die-cast 260 had a peg at one corner instead of a screw, but this would not fit Super O. The black plastic model has screws at all four corners. **Cross-references:** PW 26 260; ME 2282, 2283.

(A) Bottom fiber plate marked "NO. 260 / THE LI-ONEL CORPORATION" in white, hex nut holds plate to chassis. This is identical to late postwar Hagerstown production except for the translucent lens cap; some Hagerstown versions also had translucent caps and cannot be distinguished from this version. Type I box or Type II shrink-wrap packaging.

25   40

Exc   Mint

(B) Same as (A), but later production, no lettering on bottom fiber plate. Type II shrink-wrap packaging.

25   40

(C) Nonilluminated version: no bottom plate or electrical connections. Came in 1287 Pioneer Dockside Switcher set in 1972.

20   30

2280 BUMPERS, 1973–84

Nonilluminated, sold in packages of three; black plastic with wide clamps at rear and narrow ones at front for fastening to track; no screws required. The die-cast bumpers tended to bend O27 track inward if their screws were too tight. These much smaller bumpers replaced the reissue of the 260 in 1973. Although they look far less sturdy, they are quite a bit more realistic, and their clip system holds them in a piece of track much more stoutly than operators might think. The first versions of these accessories came with an open space behind the striking area of the bumper. Later versions had the space filled in; these are much more common. **Cross-references:** ME 2290, 12715, 12717.

(A) 1973–75, three to a package, early version with open area on top just behind bumper plate, Type I box.

5   7

	Exc	Mint
(B) 1974–84, later version with closed area.

	Exc	Mint
	3	**5**

2282 DIE-CAST BUMPER, 1983

Black-painted die-cast body that attaches to the track with screws; black plastic shock absorber, red illuminated jewel atop body. Sold in pairs in Type V box. These die-cast replicas of the postwar 260 were unusual in that they appeared as a special Fall Collector's Center piece in 1983 and were uncataloged. They were made in Hong Kong in just one run, which means they are somewhat difficult to find today, though their dark Tuscan counterparts (2283) are very common. Value per pair. **Cross-references:** PW 26, 260; ME 2283, 52039.

	25	**35**

2283 DIE-CAST BUMPER, 1984–97

Same construction as 2282 , but dark Tuscan painted die-cast body. Sold in pairs in Type III box until 1986, then found in Type VI box. After the demand for the black 2282 became evident, Fundimensions cataloged a general-use version of the sturdy 260-type bumper, this time painted in Tuscan instead of black. Like the 2282, this model was made in Hong Kong and sold in pairs, and it has sold so well that it has been a staple of the Lionel catalog since its introduction. Value per pair. **Cross-references:** PW 26, 260; ME 2282, 52039.

	CP

2290 LIGHTED BUMPERS, 1975–86

Black plastic bumper identical to late 2280 except for lamp and socket. Sold in pairs in Type III boxes. These are lighted versions of the 2280; otherwise, they are identical in construction to the second version of the 2280. Just behind the bumping surface, a socket has been installed with a subminiature red-painted screw-base lamp. This socket is connected to copper blades, which run to the center rail and the outside rail. Value per pair. **Cross-references:** ME 2280, 12715, 12717.

	10	**12**

2900 LOCKON, 1970–97

Familiar black fiber plate with two Fahnestock clips that clamps to rails for power transfer. This is the

The 2901 Track Clips kept sections of O27 gauge track securely connected. This was important for operators who didn't have a permanent layout.

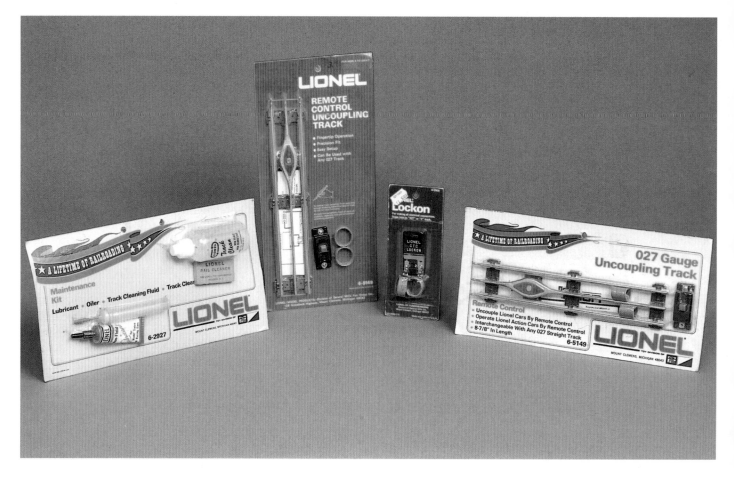

Both Model Products Corp. and Lionel Trains Inc. kept a number of ancillary items in their product lines. Among the MPC products were (left to right) 2927 Maintenance Kit, 5149 Remote Control Uncoupling Track, and 2905 Lockon and Wire

Exc   Mint

number used for the units sold in cartons in bulk, as opposed to the 2905, which includes the wire and is shrink-wrapped. If there ever was a universal possession among all Lionel collectors and operators, this would probably be it. The modern-era versions even retail the old CTC markings of the postwar years. **Cross-references:** PW CTC; ME 2905.

CP

2901 O27 TRACK CLIPS, 1970–97

Stamped metal plate that clips onto joints of O27 track to hold them secure in nonpermanent layouts. Sold in packages of 12 in Type I, II, III, or VI boxes, depending upon year of issue. The design of these little metal plates has not changed, but the stamped lettering has. Early Type I boxes (dated 1970 and some 1971) have examples with postwar lettering; late Type I boxes (some 1971 and 1972) have "BY LIONEL MPC

Exc   Mint

/ MT. CLEMENS, MICH. USA / TRACK CLIP 2901" lettering. The MPC lettering is eliminated in examples from Type II and III boxes, while those in Type VI boxes are lettered for LTI. These clips go back a long, long way, all the way back to the early 1930s and the introduction of Lionel's Winner trains, the beginning of O27 track. The O gauge clips are even older. **Cross-reference:** PW O27C-1.

CP

2905 LOCKON AND WIRE, 1974–97

Same as 2900, except includes two coils of light green wire in blister pack. Type II packages are not very common now. This is the number used for the blister-pack lockon that includes two coils of light green wire. Sold in Type II, III, or VI packages, depending upon year of issue. **Cross-references:** PW CTC; ME 2900.

CP

Exc Mint

2910 CONTACTOR, 1983–86 and 1988

Black fiber plate that clips to track; has two metal power rails used as is for O27 track or equipped with special metal extension rods for O gauge track. Reissue of postwar OTC Contactor first reissued with 9224 Louisville Horse Car of 1984 and 9290 Union Pacific Barrel Car of 1983. Subsequent versions of these cars also included this contactor. This is the modern-era number for the special OTC Contactor used to operate horse, cattle, and barrel cars. It is stamped with its new number, but it is not known if this contactor was (or is) offered for separate sale. Many postwar examples are available used in the parts market. **Cross-reference:** PW OTC.

5 8

5025 MANUMATIC UNCOUPLER, 1971–72

Black plastic clamp device that locks onto O27 track; pushing black plastic button at trackside raises two prongs that pull down the coupler shaft and uncouple the car. Included with sets, but also came packaged in Type I box as a set of three. Instructions are printed on the box itself. Before Fundimensions could come out with a revised version of the postwar 6029 uncoupler track with its magnet, the firm needed something simple and inexpensive to include with its sets for uncoupling purposes. The result was this little plastic uncoupling device, the Fundimensions equivalent of the old postwar Cam-Trol track of the late 1940s for Scout sets. The new Delrin trucks had a downward-projecting shaft that could be engaged by a double-prong device on this uncoupler. Operators pushed a plastic button after clipping the uncoupler to the track. This raised the double-prong extension just enough to catch the coupler shaft and spring the knuckle. At least, that was the theory! In practice, the device never did work very well, and soon it was jettisoned for a more efficient and traditional magnetized track section. A thumbtack (of all things!) was added to the coupler shaft to attract the magnetic force and pull the knuckle open. Most of the manumatics were included with sets, but some were sold in sets of three (!) in Type I boxes. Although the Type I boxes are hard to find today, the 5025 remains little more than a quaint cameo, even though it was a fairly clever attempt at an inexpensive uncoupling device. Value per set.

1 2

5900 AC/DC CONVERTER, 1979–83

Black rectangular box with silver lettering; connects to leads from transformer to supply DC. This small black box contained a rectifier to turn AC transformer current into DC current for the DC-only sets Fundimensions was featuring on the low end of its sales offerings in these years. Those sets did not sell very well; all Lionel motors, including the low-end can type, are now universal in nature. A similar unit was sold with Lionel's large scale trains to enable those DC-powered trains, or those offered by other G scale manufacturers, to be run with a Lionel AC transformer.

4 6

8251-50 HORN/WHISTLE CONTROLLER, 1972–74

Unmarked rectangular red or black plastic box with push button; designed to be hooked into the "hot" wire leading from a transformer to a lockon. Burned-out units have little if any value, so prices assume working order. First used for the 8204 Chesapeake & Ohio 4-4-2 steam locomotive included with the 1284 Allegheny Freight Set of 1972. This accessory was designed for the earliest Fundimensions whistles and horns, which could not be operated properly from older transformers because they would shut off at sustaining voltage and reversing switches would rattle at pickup voltage. The box contained a gated diode that opened to allow direct current (DC) into the track when the button was pushed. The trouble was that when the button was pushed only part way, the diode would stick in its closed position without operating the horn or whistle, and the transformer's voltage would burn out the diode. Most examples found today do not work because the diode is burned out. Because of this problem, Fundimensions discontinued production of electronic horns and whistles for several years. When it resumed in 1981, engineers made sure the new design worked with older transformers.

2 4

12715 ILLUMINATED BUMPERS, 1987–97

Sold two per package, Type VI box. Same design as 2290, but Tuscan in color. The 12715 and 12717 are designed identically to their Fundimensions predecessors, but they are molded in Tuscan-colored plastic rather then black. **Cross-reference:** ME 2290.

CP

12717 BUMPERS, 1987–97

Nonilluminated; same design as 2280, but Tuscan in color. Three per package, Type VI box.

CP

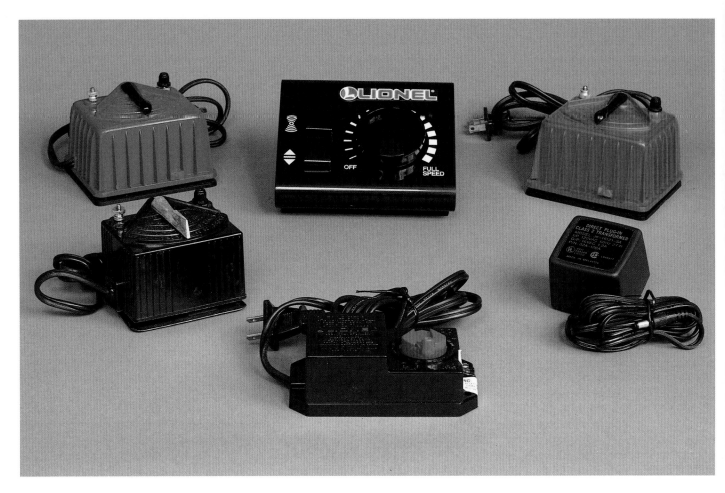

Transformers are essential items for an toy train operator. Pictured here is a sampling of the many power sources offered by MPC and LTI in an assortment of sizes and colors during the modern era.

Exc   Mint

12743 O GAUGE TRACK CLIPS, 1989–97

Narrow metal black clips packaged twelve to a Type VI box. It seems a little strange that Fundimensions never reissued the long, narrow postwar track clips, but such is the case. These clips go back even further than the O27 clips; a longer version of them was made for Standard gauge. Unlike the wide plate of the O27 clip, these clips splice together the curled-up outer sections of adjoining O gauge track ties. Two small slots cut into the bottom of the clip engage the sides of the ties. In the earlier versions, some of these clips were made with spoon-shaped grab surfaces for easy insertion and removal. **Cross-reference:** PW CO-1.

CP

15906 RAILSOUNDS TRIGGER BUTTON, 1990–92

Small black rectangular box and button with silver heat-stamped lettering. This little button in a black

Exc   Mint

square box might superficially resemble the old Fundimensions diode boxes of 1972-73, but the operation is quite different. When the button is wired into the "hot" side of the circuit going from the transformer to the track, operators can activate the locomotive bell sound built into locomotives equipped with RailSounds I. Although this button did not appear in the catalog after 1992, it has been widely available. RailSounds I has been superseded by the fully electronic, remote-controlled RailSounds II since 1994. Two types of buttons were available; one was for older Lionel transformers, and the other was specifically for the MW transformer, which was electronic.

8   12

52039 LCCA "TRACK 29" BUMPER, 1994

This was a special premium offered by the Lionel Collectors Club of America for convention attendees in 1994. Further information is needed concerning

Exc Mint

description and lettering. **Cross-references:** PW 26, 260; ME 2282, 2283.

NRS

TRANSFORMERS AND POWER SOURCES

The transformer is perhaps the single most basic tool of any model railroading system. The whole operation of a layout depends upon the kind of current the transformer produces and the configuration of its controls. Lionel's transformers have always been simple devices—until now, with the introduction of very sophisticated electronic control systems. Even with electronic systems, however, the basic task of the transformer has always been to convert household electric current into low-voltage current that will operate trains in complete safety. They do so by means of the principle of induction; household current passes through one primary coil, where a part of it is induced into a second coil that supplies the low-voltage current. By tapping into this secondary coil with a variable rheostat, the passage of the current can be controlled for a train's speed and an accessory's operation.

Lionel's first transformers were not always convenient. Until 1938, the firm issued transformers with five or six "click" stops, and every time current was interrupted by passing from one stop to the other, the current would be interrupted and the locomotive's reversing switch triggered—scarcely a way to run a model railroad smoothly. Lionel solved this problem with a separate rheostat device, but it wasn't very convenient to use and used asbestos for insulation, hardly a safe practice today. The continuously variable speed controls of the 1938 and later units were much easier to use.

However, the rheostat controls were not the main issue in transformers; that issue was power. As each Lionel layout expanded, more and more power was needed to control and run the vast number of trains and accessories available. Therefore, during the postwar era Lionel's transformers ranged all the way from basic 25-watt affairs included with small starter sets to the magnificent 275-watt ZW model, capable of running four trains and still a great favorite with operators not infatuated with the new generation of electronic control systems. Such powerful transformers could, and did, operate large toy train empires in the postwar world.

If power was a solution for postwar Lionel, it became a problem for Fundimensions in its earliest years. In the late 1960s and early '70s, America became safety conscious with its toys, and as part of that

phenomenon the Occupational and Safety Hazard Administration (better known as OSHA), issued new and very restrictive guidelines for electricity-producing devices. Among these guidelines were standards for toy train transformers that prohibited the manufacture of any transformer with more than 100 watts of power capacity. These restrictions painted both Fundimensions and Lionel railroaders into a corner, leaving the latter to find high-power transformers made before OSHA's restrictions. The recipe of fixed supply and accelerated demand ensured that the price of large postwar transformers would climb steadily.

That wasn't the only problem posed by restrictive safety guidelines in the early 1970s. In 1972 Fundimensions faced a mandated redesign of the wall plugs for transformers into a new "safety" design. This would not have been much of a problem except for two elements: (1) There was a severe shortage of copper wire that year; and (2) Canadian safety standards differed from American ones, and all new transformers had to meet both standards. This state of affairs resulted in some anxious moments for Fundimensions, as internal documents clearly show. At stake was the transformer supply for the 1972 sets slated to meet an increased demand for the trains during the holiday season. It took some last-minute designs and a lot of scrambling, but eventually Fundimensions proved itself equal to the challenge, although the firm could not make as many sets as it wished.

During the Fundimensions years, no truly new transformer designs were attempted until the introduction of the all-electronic MW unit at the very end of that time. This transformer, later modified into the RS-1 by Lionel Trains Inc., was underpowered and only partially successful. Eventually, LTI publicized an attempt to market a new version of the postwar ZW to be called the ZW-II. To comply with eased transformer restrictions, the company planned to market this new and improved ZW as a hobbyist transformer instead of a toy. However, the new ZW was never marketed for two reasons. The first was that it could not be made inexpensively enough to compete with the postwar ZWs already available through extensive dealer and operator rebuilding and a thriving spare parts market. The second reason was that the development of a fully electronic and radically different train control system was about to consign the ZW and its ilk to the dinosaur age of Lionel railroading.

In 1994 LTI and Liontech, a subsidiary, introduced the revolutionary TrainMaster Control System, which changed the rules of Lionel operation. In the past, the only way an operator could get true control over multiple-train operation was to secure a twin-throttle transformer such as the KW or ZW and use it with a cab

Exc   Mint

control system using insulated track blocks and switches with A-B-Center off positions. With the new system, the power supply, electronic command center, and new, fully programmable walkaround throttle and control unit were all separate entities.

This system gives operators complete remote control over trains, sound systems, and even accessories from one master control unit, a huge advance over the many buttons and switches of the past. Even the small transformers included with Lionel's starter sets include a separate wall plug for power and a controller unit with much more flexibility than the integrated transformers of the past. These new transformer systems give Lionel the same operational advantages HO and other scale enthusiasts have enjoyed with their DC-powered trains, especially the option to run a Lionel railroad as a dispatcher on a real railroad would, complete with assignment cards and assistant operators. The new control system promises to be a tremendous advantage for Lionel's modular layout clubs as well as the individual operator.

Still, the new age of Lionel's control systems should not obscure the highly successful past of its transformer designs. They were successful because they were simple, and for that reason it is likely that KWs, ZWs, and many other old warhorses from Lionel's stable will be with us for a very long time.

Prior to about 1975, wattage outputs were measured by "peak power" ratings. Such ratings were not realistic because they were predicated upon maximum output under full load, a condition seldom encountered in operation, and allowed for highly inflated wattage numbers. For example, the fabled Lionel ZW was measured at 275 watts in peak power.

After the mid-1970s, the "wattage war" among stereo component manufacturers led to some reforms in stated power ratings. Now wattage output is measured by RMS (Root Mean Square) output. This rating is predicated upon continuous output under normal conditions and loads, which is a more realistic measure of power output. That 275-watt peak power ZW actually puts out about 180 watts RMS power.

Recently Lionel announced the marketing of a new Power Master transformer (with separate controller) that will put out 135 watts RMS power; this is not too far removed from the ZW. Another manufacturer has announced the marketing of a 190-watt RMS transformer! That would be more powerful than even the ZW, although it remains to be seen whether the device can be marketed legally or successfully because of regulations issued by the Consumer Products Safety Commission. The disparity between peak power

wattages of postwar (and early MPC) transformers and the RMS measurements of later days must be considered in any comparison of power sources for Lionel trains.

FUNDIMENSIONS PRODUCTION

4044 TRANSFORMER, 1970–71

Forty-five-watt transformer, black and brown marbled plastic case, metal lever controls speed, no forward-reverse button, two binding posts, older type of wall plug. The case is very unusual, and no doubt several examples of this transformer have been found with all-black ones, a more normal configuration. Marbled plastic is recycled material, and the last time it was used came in the early 1950s during the Korean War for whistle casings for tenders and whistle shacks. It is not certain if the cases used for 4044s were newly made or leftover cases from a much earlier production period; reader comments are requested. **Cross-references:** PW 1045; ME 4045.

10   15

4045 SAFETY TRANSFORMER, 1970–71

Forty-five-watt transformer, black case, variable AC output, metal lever controls speed, automatic circuit breaker, two binding posts with one serving as forward and reverse button. Despite its name, this model still had the older type of wall plug; the newer plugs do not show up until 1972. It is possible that Fundimensions wanted to draw attention to the presence of a circuit breaker, though it was also present in the 4044. The major difference between this and the 4044 was the use of one binding post as a forward-reverse button; that became Fundimensions' standard practice in its smaller set transformers. Separate sales of small transformers began with the 4050 model. **Cross-references:** PW 1045; ME 4044.

10   15

4050 SAFETY TRANSFORMER, 1972–79

Fifty-watt transformer, can be found with either metal or plastic lever. Has flat-surfaced safety plug and reinforced strain-relief grommet where plug enters transformer. Made with both blue cases and metal control levers (earlier production) and red cases with black plastic control levers (later production). This was the first small transformer offered by Fundimensions for separate sale. As related in the introduction, interoffice correspondence reveals that Lionel had a difficult time remanufacturing this transformer, the back-

The 4060 Power Master transformer boasted a strong output of power for so small a transformer. It featured fixed AC and variable DC output.

Exc   Mint

bone of its starter sets. Once a successful design was approved, Lionel had trouble securing the electric cords and plugs needed. **Cross-references:** PW 1043; ME 4150, 4250, 4651.

10   15

4060 POWER MASTER, 1980–93

Black case, fixed AC and variable DC output, direction reverse switch, automatic circuit breaker. The resemblance of this model to the Fundimensions AC transformers is only superficial. The 4060 is more like an HO power pack than a typical Lionel transformer, and it has a good output for so small a unit. The control lever varies direct current to the tracks, while there are also fixed-voltage AC posts to the accessories. The binding posts are in pairs at the corners of the case, which represents an unusual arrangement. A small red sliding switch reverses the DC to the train. **Cross-references:** ME 4065, 4851.

12   20

4065 DC HOBBY TRANSFORMER, 1981–83

Black plastic case, white lettering, red speed control lever, reversing switch, 0–18 volts DC, 19 volts AC. This was the DC transformer included with Fundimensions' experiments with DC-powered trains in the early 1980s. Other than from cosmetics, commentary is necessary regarding differences be-

Exc   Mint

tween the 4065 and the 4060. **Cross-references:** ME 4060, 4851.

3   4

4090 POWER MASTER, 1970–81 and 1983

Ninety-watt transformer with two red levers (right controls speed, left controls direction and whistle; two variable and two fixed voltage taps atop transformer face, automatic circuit breaker, silver press-on label on transformer face identical to 1044 except for Fundimensions logo. This model is a direct remake of the postwar 1044, which itself is derived from the 1033, quite possibly the most dependable single-throttle transformer ever manufactured by Lionel. Its voltage ranges are identical to the 1044's: as many as 19 volts AC for the train and 11-volt fixed posts for accessories. It also has the old whistle control employing a copper-oxide disk rectifier for the direct current needed for the whistle. Most of these units were sold as separate-sale items, but in the early 1970s some turned up in large outfits, including the 1187 Illinois Central Service Station Set from 1971. **Cross-references:** PW 1033, 1044.

50   60

4125 TRANSFORMER, 1972

Twenty-five-watt transformer; typically light blue case, though light maroon ones have been reported; no

The 4090 Power Master transformer represented the return of the well-known 1044 from the postwar years. The 4090 was available as a separate-sale item as well as a set component.

Exc Mint

direction control post; metal lever for speed control. This very basic transformer was the first to incorporate the new safety cord and plug; it was found with the less expensive starter sets in 1972, such as the 1287 Pioneer Dockside Switcher. **Cross-reference:** PW 1101.

7 10

4150 MULTIVOLT TOY TRANSFORMER, 1972–73 and 1975–77

Fifty-watt transformer; AC output, blue plastic case, bright metal or black plastic speed control lever. Although nominally a 50-watt model identical to the earlier 4050, this transformer also measured output in volts AC instead of wattage, which may account for the different number. **Cross-references:** PW 1043; ME 4050, 4250, 4651.

15 20

4250 TRAIN MASTER TRANSFORMER, 1973

Fifty-watt nominal output; blue plastic case with black plastic speed control lever. We are not certain

Exc Mint

why this transformer, which essentially was identical to the 4050 and 4150, used a different number for this year only. Reader comments are needed. **Cross-references:** PW 1043; ME 4050, 4150, 4651.

15 20

4651 TRAIN MASTER TRANSFORMER, 1978–79

Red plastic case, black plastic lever controls speed, two posts with button on one post for forward and reverse, automatic circuit breaker. This is the successor number to the 4150, with the only apparent difference being that the case measures output in volts AC, not wattage. **Cross-references:** PW 1043; ME 4050, 4150, 4250.

10 15

4690 TYPE MW TRANSFORMER, 1986–89

Black metal case, orange knobs and buttons, red, white, and blue Lionel logo, white lettering. Power-off switch (incredibly, the first in any Lionel transformer),

The 4690 Type MW was the first Lionel transformer to include a power-off switch. It was cataloged at the end of the Fundimensions years and into the initial LTI years.

Exc   Mint

0–17 volts AC output, variable accessory voltage knob can also be used to power a second train; solid-state construction, variable intensity indicator lights for track and accessory lines, power-on light, horn/whistle, and directional buttons, circuit breaker. Lionel's first truly modern transformer; it resembles those issued previously by Model Power and Tech II. This all-new electronic model was cataloged at the end of the Fundimensions years (in fact, during its brief spin-off to Kenner-Parker Toys) and finally put Lionel on the road to modern power for its trains. The 4690 was only partially successful because it was limited to one-train operation and even then was somewhat underpowered, but it was the first sign of modernization for Lionel's power systems. It was replaced by the RS-1 in 1990, essentially similar but with an added control for RailSounds I. This in turn was replaced by the new TrainMaster Control System in 1994. **Cross-reference:** ME 12780.

75   95

Exc   Mint

4851 DC TRANSFORMER, 1985–91 and 1994

Output of 15 volts AC, red case, black plastic handle. Essentially similar to previous small DC transformers issued by Fundimensions. The 4851 was used for many inexpensive special sets, including the 11756 Hawthorne Freight Flyer from 1987–88 and the 11721 Mickey's World Tour Train from 1991. **Cross-references:** ME 4060, 4065.

3   4

4870   HOBBY TRANSFORMER AND THROTTLE CONTROL, 1977–78

Consists of two pieces: a small black plastic wall-plug AC transformer and a red plastic throttle control. Transformer marked "Made In Taiwan", but throttle control marked "Mt. Clemens, Mich." This was an unusual (for Lionel) DC separate transformer and control unit used for the 1860 and 1862 Workin' On The Railroad sets cataloged in 1978. Curiously, it was a predecessor of the AC units later marketed by LTI that also feature a two-piece arrangement. The 4870 is similar to those controllers found in slot-car sets.

3   4

LIONEL TRAINS INC. PRODUCTION

12780 RS-1 TRANSFORMER, 1990–93

Black sheet-metal case with white lettering and LTI's Lionel logo; red control knobs with white lettering and offset handles. This model is essentially identical to the 4690 MW transformer, except for its RailSounds I button, which was added to activate the new sound system, and its redesigned throttle knobs with handles. The trouble with this and the earlier MW is that once the second knob for accessories is used for a second train, no provision is available for accessory operation. In effect, this limits the 4690 and

12780 transformers to single-train operation. **Cross-reference:** ME 4690.

100   150

12790 ZW II TRANSFORMER, 1992

This new version of the old favorite among Lionel operators, the ZW, was scheduled for early 1992, but cataloged in 1991. It was to have all the features of the postwar ZW transformer, though newer electronic practices were to replace older technology, including a diode-controlled whistle-horn switch instead of the old copper-oxide rectifier disks. Its black casing was to be styled like the original ZW, but a RailSounds I activation button would have been added. However, this transformer was never marketed. Opinions differ as to why; one story is that OSHA frowned on the high output wattage even though the transformer was to be designated as a hobbyist's item, not a toy. Apparently the resemblance to the old unit was a sticking point. Another reason, perhaps a bit more credible, is that

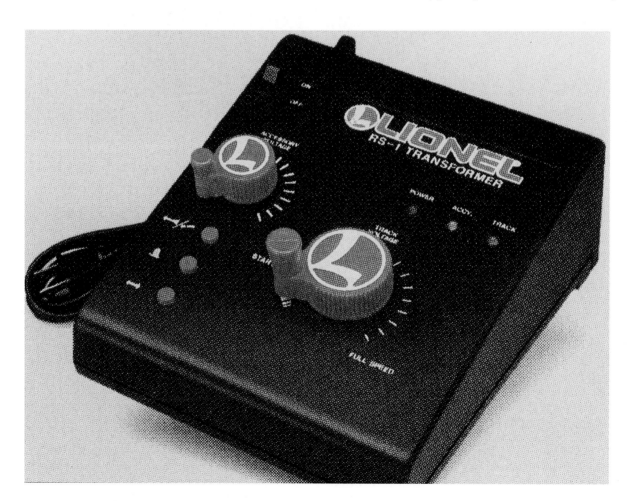

The 12780 RS-1, shown here as illustrated in the 1991 Lionel Trains Inc. catalog, updated the 4690 MW by adding a button to control RailSounds I.

The big news circulating among toy train operators in 1991 was talk that Lionel planned to revise the famed postwar ZW transformer for release the next year. However, this rumor never became reality because the 12790 ZW II would have been competing with postwar transformers for modelers' dollars. In addition, the ZW II looked too much like its predecessor and may have violated standards on output wattage established by the Occupational Hazards Safety Agency.

Exc   Mint

the ZW II would have been much too expensive in competition with the many older ZWs and parts on the market. We now also know that Lionel's thoughts about power control were turning in a new and revolutionary direction with the TrainMaster Control System. **Cross-reference:** PW ZW-R.

Not Manufactured

12849 AC CONTROLLER WITH WALL PACK, 1994

Standard high-to-low voltage wall plug to transform house current; black controller case features large dial with white markings and circle-L logo; includes whistle/horn control and directional button. This separate wall transformer and control unit was intended by Lionel to accompany starter sets. Unfortunately, it had a high failure rate because of a

Exc   Mint

design flaw in the controller unit. The 12849 was quickly replaced by the redesigned but outwardly identical 12885 unit, which was more powerful and reliable. Value assumes unit is in working order. **Cross-reference:** ME 12885.

10   15

12866 PH-1 POWER HOUSE POWER SUPPLY, 1994–97

Black-finned rectangular box transformer designed solely for output of 135 watts RMS. On-off switch, circuit breaker light, and inset Lionel logo and lettering. This and the units that follow are part of the Train-Master Control System, a modular power and control system of immense flexibility and versatility unlike anything Lionel has offered before. In fact, one of the characteristics of this system is that it is so unlike

The revolutionary TrainMaster Control System, offering toy train enthusiasts command control for their layouts, consists of the 12866 PH-1 Power House, 12867 PM-1 Power Master, 12868 CAB-1 Wireless Remote Control, and 12890 Big Red switch. The units were introduced to the hobby in the 1995 catalog.

Exc   Mint

Lionel! It is meant to appeal to a new audience of sophisticated operators capable of understanding and using this system to its greatest potential. It is even compatible with computer programs, thanks to a plug that was built into the PM-1 Power Master Base.

This is not the place to discuss the operating capabilities of the system in any detail. That has already been done, quite brilliantly, by Peter Riddle in the third volume of his excellent series, *Wiring Your Lionel Layout* (Kalmbach Publishing Co.). However, some informed speculation may be appropriate here. The key question with the TrainMaster Control System is whether it will catch on with operators already used to such electronic sophistry or become another technically brilliant but ultimately impractical Lionel option such as Rail Scope. Interestingly enough, in the latest Lionel accessory catalog, there's a marketing research card, part of which deals with the new system. One question asks, "Will you purchase a system? If no, why not?" The choices given are, interestingly, "cost," "complexity," and "prefer transformer." The TrainMaster is a very expensive system, which will shut out all but the most serious operators. In short, owners of old ZWs need not put away their transformers just yet!

CP

12867 PM-1 POWER MASTER BASE, 1994–97

Dark gray rectangular box with variable and fixed output settings; Lionel logo and script inlaid atop box. This device offers the controlling capacity for the power from either a conventional transformer or the 12866 PH-1 Power House Power Supply. It is meant to be used with the 12868 CAB-1 Remote Control Unit. Multiple units can be used on a railroad for different functions or different insulated blocks.

CP

12868 CAB-1 REMOTE CONTROLLER, 1994–97

Dark gray control box with red rotary throttle control and Lionel logo and typescript; retractable antenna achieves range of control signals; takes four AA alkaline batteries. The 12868 is a remote wireless walkaround throttle and controller of considerable complexity and ingenuity. Through a number keypad, individual locomotives on a layout can be remotely

Though committed to promoting the Train-Master Control System, LTI continued to improve its line of traditional transformers. As proof, it brought out the 12880 Power Station in 1995.

Exc Mint

activated and controlled without interfering with any other operations. Through other connections, switches can be thrown and accessories activated. The battery-powered unit has a claimed range of 150 feet!

CP

2880 POWER STATION POWER SUPPLY, 1995–97

Black PH-1 rectangular box and separate black box with red rotary speed control and buttons with white graduated markings, circle-L logo and lettering, triple-smokestack Power House logo in black, red, and white; 135-watt RMS power output. This two-piece traditional transformer, which isn't part of the TrainMaster Control System, includes a 12866 PH-1 Power House Power Supply and a separate control box resembling the earlier RM-1 transformer. It has been given a new number and extensively redesigned for 1997. **Cross-reference:** ME 12938.

CP

Exc Mint

12885 LIONEL 40-WATT CONTROL SYSTEM, 1995–96

Two separate units, one to reduce the 120-volt current, the other to serve as a controller. The first is a black wall unit, and the second has a large black rotary dial with white markings, Lionel logo and script and white-marked bell/whistle and directional buttons. Output is 3 amps, 40 watts RMS. This traditional transformer with separate controller is essentially an improved version of the earlier 12849 unit, which was not altogether satisfactory. This unit, which isn't part of the TrainMaster Control System, has a redesigned rheostat, bell/whistle button, directional button, and green pilot lamp that brightens with increased power output. **Cross-reference:** ME 12849.

CP

12890 LIONEL "BIG RED SWITCH," 1994–97

Large red button on black base with connecting wire and white circle-L logo. When this large button is plugged into the CAB-1 remote unit, it activates any command sent by the CAB-1 and repeats the command with each push. This device enables children to activate commands programmed into the system by an adult.

CP

12893 POWER MASTER ADAPTER CABLE, 1994–97

Black cable with plug-in connectors at one end and wire terminals at other to connect traditional transformer to TrainMaster System. This cable enables the PM-1 Power Master to be plugged into a traditional transformer instead of the PH-1 Power House unit. In this way, owners of the ZW and other older transformers can use those units to power the TrainMaster.

CP

12911 TRAINMASTER COMMAND BASE, 1994–97

Same shape and appearance as 12867, except color of unit is black instead of dark gray. Requires a wall power unit, which is included. This device is similar to the PM-1 Power Master; however, unlike that unit, the 12911 is designed to activate command-equipped Lionel locomotives with RailSounds II and the SC1 Switch and Accessory Controller.

CP

12914 SC-1 SWITCH AND ACCESSORY CONTROLLER, 1995–97

Dark gray rectangular box with light gray circle-L logo; four sets of screw terminals for switch wires and two sets for accessory leads. The 12914 consists of a set of terminals that work with the Command Base and the CAB-1 Controller. Each controller activates as many as four turnouts and two accessories; they can be installed in multiples on a layout.

CP

12938 POWER STATION–POWER HOUSE SET, 1997

Power supply resembles that of 12866; controller is squared black box with center speed knob embossed with circle-L logo. Two small push buttons on left of box and one on right; illuminated green Lionel lettering at top front increases in intensity with output, much like the old LW transformer dial. This two-piece traditional transformer appears to be a substantially

redesigned version of the 12880. Like its predecessor, it includes a 12866 Power House unit, but the controller unit appears to be completely different in cosmetics if not in circuitry. The case of the controller is black, with a center knob for speed control and three push buttons for whistle, horn, and directional functions. Its output is 8 amps and 135 watts RMS. **Cross-reference:** ME 12880.

NRS

12939 POWER GRID–POWER HOUSE SET, 1997

Like the 12938, this accessory is accompanied by a 12866 Power House unit. The 12939 is designed to power accessories with fixed voltages instead of the varying voltages used by the trains themselves. Provisions are included for 10-, 12-, 14-, and 16-volt outputs. Controller is a rectangular box lacking a throttle control but including clips for four different accessory voltages. Large illuminated Lionel lettering at top of front is constantly lighted.

NRS

O27 GAUGE TRACK, 1970–97

Lionel's lightweight O27 gauge track, by a wide margin the most popular size of track made by Lionel, has a history dating to 1930, when it was introduced as part of the inexpensive, Depression-inspired Winner Line. Gradually this track became Lionel's price-leader track, included in inexpensive ready-to-run sets during the entire postwar period and throughout the modern era to this day. Even though the 27-inch radius of this track is very tight, it will handle all but the largest Lionel locomotives and rolling stock.

The chief asset of O27 track is its low price, and not just as new track. Used O27 track is available in staggering quantities at train shows and shops, offering a real bargain for Lionel railroaders. Working against this track is its inability to accommodate high speeds and larger equipment, and its fragility, especially the switches. Lionel's prewar and postwar 1121 and 1122E O27 switches were durable, efficient units, but the redesigned 5121 and 5122 units of the modern era are flimsy, though they work reasonably well. The chief reason for this fragility is the delicate plastic drive pin connecting the movable frog rail to the solenoid. Once this pin is broken, the switch cannot be repaired. Unfortunately, this is also true of the newer 5167-5168 wide-radius versions.

Most seasoned operators who use O27 gauge look for the 1122E versions, which are also illuminated (un-

The range of track available from Fundimensions was evident in the 1978 catalog.

like the modern-era versions). If the nonderailing feature is unnecessary, the pre-1952 1121 models are an even sturdier choice. Another track that has misled operators is the 12746 Operating Track. Lionel initially implied that it would operate any animated car; in fact, the 12746 is too small to accommodate the sliding shoes of O gauge operating cars.

5012 CURVED TRACK, 1970–91

Four pieces on a card; shrink-wrap packaging varies with production year. **Cross-reference:** PW 1013.

	Exc	Mint
	2.20	3.50

5013 CURVED TRACK, 1970–97

Single piece of track. **Cross-reference:** PW 1013.
CP

5014 HALF-CURVED TRACK, 1970–97

Single piece of track. **Cross-reference:** PW 1014.
CP

5016 THREE-FOOT STRAIGHT SECTION, 1987

This track was discontinued and replaced by the 5024 when LTI realized that its 36" length was longer than the four single pieces it was supposed to replace.
2.25

5017 STRAIGHT TRACK, 1980–83

Four pieces on a card. **Cross-reference:** PW 1017.
3.50

5018 STRAIGHT TRACK, 1980–97

Single piece of track. **Cross-reference:** PW 1017.
CP

5019 HALF-STRAIGHT TRACK, 1980–97

Single piece of track. **Cross-reference:** PW 1018.
CP

5020 90-DEGREE CROSSOVER, 1980–97

Single piece of track. **Cross-reference:** PW 1020.
CP

5023 45-DEGREE CROSSOVER, 1980–97

Single piece of track. **Cross-references:** PW 1023; ME 5823.
CP

Crossovers, such as the 5023 45-Degree, have long been cataloged in the Lionel line.

Exc   Mint

5024 STRAIGHT TRACK, 1980–96

Single piece of 35" track.

CP

5025 MANUMATIC UNCOUPLER, 1971–75

Small Type I box with three black plastic uncoupling devices that clamp to track. Pushing a button raises two extensions between the rails; these are supposed to catch the coupler disks and pull them down. As a rule, these uncouplers do not work well. Packed three to a box; instructions printed on the box.

2   3

5030 TRACK EXPANDER SET, 1972

Canadian catalog refers to this as Switch Layout Expander Set. Type I box with pair of manual switches, two sections of curved O27 track, and six sections of straight O27 track. Made for distribution in Canada by Parker Brothers.

25   35

5030 LAYOUT BUILDER SET, 1978–80 and 1983

Pair of manual switches, two sections of curved O27 track, and six sections of straight O27 track. American production of Track Expander Set.

20   30

Exc   Mint

5033 CURVED TRACK, 1980–97

Bulk packed in cartons of 100 pieces, but sold individually. **Cross-reference:** PW 1013.

CP

5038 STRAIGHT TRACK, 1980–97

Bulk packed in cartons of 100 pieces, but sold individually. **Cross-reference:** PW 1018.

CP

5041 O27 INSULATOR PINS, 1980–97

Pack of twelve pins. **Cross-reference:** PW 1122-234.

CP

5042 O27 STEEL PINS, 1980–97

Pack of twelve pins. Earlier versions were hollow and bent easily; later production features solid pins. **Cross-reference:** PW 1013-17.

CP

5044 O42 CURVED TRACK BALLAST PIECE, 1987–88

Although these pieces gave a realistic look to the track, they were made with hollows for the track ties

	Exc	Mint

and thus were very fragile. They did not sell well because operators preferred other ballast pieces on the market. Price per piece.

2.25

5045 O27 WIDE-RADIUS CURVED TRACK BALLAST PIECE, 1987–88

Molded gray flexible rubber ballast.

2.25

5046 O27 CURVED TRACK BALLAST PIECE, 1987–88

Molded gray flexible rubber ballast.

2.25

	Exc	Mint

5047 O27 STRAIGHT TRACK BALLAST PIECE, 1987–88

Molded gray flexible rubber ballast.

2.25

5049 O42 CURVED TRACK, 1988–97

Twelve sections make a 42"-diameter circle.

CP

5113 O54 WIDE-RADIUS TRACK, 1988–97

Sixteen sections make a 54"-diameter circle.

CP

ADD TRACK

REMOTE SWITCHES
Off-track, remote control unit diverts train.
LEFT SWITCH — 6-5121
RIGHT SWITCH — 6-5122
SWITCH SET — 6-5125
Set includes one right-hand and one left-hand remote switch plus controllers

MANUAL SWITCHES
Flip of lever on switch diverts train.
LEFT SWITCH — 6-5021
RIGHT SWITCH — 6-5022
SWITCH SET — 6-5027
Set includes one right-hand and one left-hand manual switch.

REMOTE CONTROL TRACK
Allows remote uncoupling and activation of operating cars by off-track remote control unit.   6-5149

STRAIGHT TRACK
HALF STRAIGHT — 6-5019
FULL STRAIGHT — 6-5018
CARD OF FOUR
FULL STRAIGHT — 6-5017

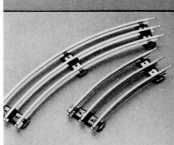

CURVE TRACK
HALF CURVE — 6-5014
FULL CURVE — 6-5013
CARD OF FOUR
CURVE TRACK — 6-5012

90° CROSSING
The perfect crossing for standard figure-8 layouts. Realistic track bed.
6-5020

LAYOUT BUILDER SET
Provides opportunity to create a variety of new track layouts. Includes two manual switches, two sections of curved track and six sections of straight track.
6-5030

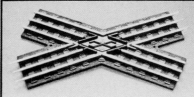

45° CROSSING
For use in making long, extended figure-8 layouts. Realistic track bed.
6-5023

'O' GAUGE TRACK
FULL CURVED TRACK — 6-5501
10⅞" in length.
FULL STRAIGHT TRACK — 6-5500
10" in length.

The 5030 Layout Builder Set, cataloged in 1978–80 and 1983, contained an assortment of track sure to help an operator assemble an enjoyable model railroad.

Straight and curved pieces of ballasted roadbed were added to the Lionel line in 1987.

	Exc	Mint

5149 REMOTE CONTROL UNCOUPLING TRACK, 1971–97

This unit lacks the power blades for remote-controlled cars; it includes a small push button and wires. Earlier versions can be found in Types I, II, or III shrink-wrap packaging; current production uses Type V shrink-wrap. Type I packaging is difficult to find. **Cross-reference: PW 6029.**

CP

12746 O27 OPERATING/UNCOUPLING TRACK, 1989–97

Essentially identical to postwar 6019. Catalog and box claim O gauge cars can be operated on this track, but in practice it is too short for many O gauge milk cars, barrel cars, and so forth. Comes in Type V box.

CP

O27 GAUGE SWITCHES, 1970–97

5021 MANUAL SWITCH, 1970–97

Left-hand switch; earliest version in Type I Banner Box hard to find.

CP

	Exc	Mint

5022 MANUAL SWITCH, 1970–97

Right-hand switch.

CP

5027 PAIR MANUAL SWITCHES, 1970–87

Pair consists of one 5021 and one 5022 switches.

20   35

5090 THREE PAIR MANUAL SWITCHES, 1983

Three each of 5021 and 5022 switches.

75   100

5121 REMOTE SWITCH, 1970–97

Left-hand, nonilluminated switch; single nonilluminated controller. **Cross-reference: PW 1122E.**

CP

5122 REMOTE SWITCH, 1970–97

Right-hand, nonilluminated switch; single nonilluminated controller. **Cross-reference: PW 1122E.**

CP

	Exc	Mint

5125 PAIR REMOTE SWITCHES, 1970–87

Pair consists of one 5121 and one 5122 switches, two individual controllers. **Cross-reference:** PW 1122E.

30 45

5167 O42 WIDE-RADIUS REMOTE SWITCH, 1990–97

Left-hand switch; essentially similar in construction to regular switch.

CP

5168 O42 WIDE-RADIUS REMOTE SWITCH, 1990–97

Right-hand switch; essentially similar in construction to regular switch.

CP

5823 45-DEGREE CROSSOVER, 1970–77

Type I or Type II shrink-wrap packaging, comes in light brown or dark brown base. Number changed in 1978 to 5023, which is identical except with Type III and then Type V shrink-wrap. **Cross-references:** PW 1023; ME 5023.

6 8

	Exc	Mint

O GAUGE TRACK, SWITCHES, AND UNCOUPLERS, 1970–97

Lionel's O gauge track has a long and distinguished history dating back to 1915, when the company still was young. Of course, this gauge didn't originate with Lionel. It was made by Ives as well as Märklin before 1900. O gauge track has the same width between the rails as O27 gauge, but it is higher and more substantially constructed than O27 Gauge, and therefore tends to be more expensive.

Even with the proliferation of O gauge track made by GarGraves, MDK Electric Trains, and other manufacturers, Lionel's has always been the track of choice for serious operators because of its rugged construction and plentiful supply. The manual and remote switches, dating back to the prewar 011 models, have been just as durable as the track itself. Operators still like to use pairs of the postwar 022 models, since they are easily found in excellent condition for about the price of new units.

550C CURVED TRACK, 1970

Single piece of 10⅞"-long track; this was the initial number designation for O gauge track until the following year, when it was changed to 5500. **Cross-references:** PW OC; ME 5500, 5510.

1.75

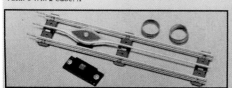

6-65149 REMOTE UNCOUPLING TRACK
Uncouples all cars equipped with operating knuckle couplers by remote control. Also activates operating cars. 8¾" long.
Pack: 6 Wt.: 2 Cube: .1

6-12746 027 OPERATING UNCOUPLING TRACK
This track allows operation of "O" Gauge operating cars on 027 layouts. Milk cars, cattle cars and other, older designs can now work on your 027 layouts. 8¾" long.
Pack: 6 Wt.: 5 Cube: .8

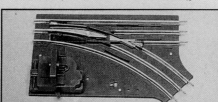

027 Manual Switches allow for more interesting layouts, such as track sidings, train switching yards or ovals within ovals. The straight track section is 8¾", the curved track section is 9⅝".

6-65022 MANUAL SWITCH, RIGHT HAND
Pack: 12 Wt.: 12 Cube: 1.2
6-65021 MANUAL SWITCH, LEFT HAND
Pack: 12 Wt.: 12 Cube: 1.2

027 Remote Switches add the layout variety of manual switches and the convenience of remote control. The straight track section is 8¾", the curved track section is 9⅝".

6-65121 REMOTE SWITCH, LEFT HAND
Pack: 6 Wt.: 6 Cube: .6

6-65122 REMOTE SWITCH, RIGHT HAND
Pack: 6 Wt.: 6 Cube: .6

Lionel 042 Remote Switches are equipped with controllers with realistic throw-type switches, 027 profile rails, and easy-to-see red/green switch post markers. The straight track section is 13⅝", the curved track section is 10⁵⁄₁₆."

6-65168 042 REMOTE SWITCH, RIGHT HAND
Pack: 6 Wt.: 8 Cube: .8
6-65167 042 REMOTE SWITCH, LEFT HAND
Pack: 6 Wt.: 8 Cube: .8

Various manual and remote-controlled left- and right-hand switches were necessary parts of the modern-era line right from the start in 1970.

	Exc	Mint

550S STRAIGHT TRACK, 1970

Single piece of 10"-long track. **Cross-references:** PW OS; ME 5501.

1.75

UCS REMOTE-CONTROL TRACK, 1970

Accessory rails, two-button controller, magnet. These were leftover postwar units marketed by Model Products Corp. **Cross-references:** PW UCS; ME 5502, 5530.

15   20

5500 STRAIGHT TRACK, 1971–97

Single piece of 10"-long track. **Cross-references:** PW OS; ME 550S.

CP

5501 CURVED TRACK, 1971–97

Single piece of 10⅞"-long track. **Cross-references:** PW OS; ME 550S.

CP

5502 REMOTE-CONTROL TRACK, 1971

Length is 10". Differences between this track and the current 5530 model are not certain. **Cross-references:** PW UCS; ME UCS, 5530.

12   16

5504 HALF CURVED SECTION, 1971–97

Single piece of track. **Cross-reference:** PW TOC

CP

5505 HALF STRAIGHT SECTION, 1971–97

Single half-section of track. **Cross-reference:** PW TOS.

CP

5510 CURVED TRACK, 1971–97

Single piece of track. **Cross-references:** PW OC; ME 550C, 5501.

CP

5520 90-DEGREE CROSSOVER, 1971

Single piece of track; postwar leftovers marketed under this number by Model Products Corp. **Cross-references:** PW 020; ME 5540.

12   14

5522 THREE-FOOT STRAIGHT SECTION, 1987

This 36"-long section of straight track was hurriedly replaced by the 5523 when LTI realized that it was not an exact-length replacement for four regular O gauge sections.

4   6

5523 EXTRA-LONG STRAIGHT SECTION, 1988–97

This 40"-long section of straight track properly replaces four regular O gauge sections.

CP

5530 REMOTE UNCOUPLING SECTION, 1988–97

This accessory and its two-button controller come in a Classic Type V box. **Cross-references:** PW UCS; ME UCS, 5502.

CP

5540 90-DEGREE CROSSOVER, 1988–97

This single section of track comes in Classic Type V box. **Cross-references:** PW 020; ME 5520.

CP

5543 INSULATOR PINS, 1980–96

Pack of twelve pins; white nylon is early production; black plastic is late production. **Cross-reference:** PW T011-43.

CP

5545 45-DEGREE CROSSOVER, 1982–97

Single piece of track. **Cross-reference:** PW 020X.

CP

5551 STEEL PINS, 1970–97

Pack of twelve pins; envelope design varies with year of production. **Cross-reference:** PW 1013-42.

CP

Exc   Mint

5560   WIDE-RADIUS CURVED TRACK BALLAST PIECE, 1987–88

Gray molded rubber piece with cut-outs for track ties. A slow seller because of its delicate construction. There was no sound deadening ability, since the ties of the track remained in contact with the platform, unlike American Flyer's postwar ballast pieces, in which the ties were cushioned by another layer of rubber.

2.25

5561   CURVED TRACK BALLAST PIECE, 1987–88

Molded gray flexible rubber ballast.

2.25

5562   STRAIGHT TRACK BALLAST PIECE, 1987–88

Molded gray flexible rubber ballast.

2.25

5572   O72 WIDE-RADIUS TRACK, 1988–97

Sixteen sections make a 72"-diameter circle. **Cross-reference:** PW 760.

CP

12840   INSULATED TRACK SECTION, 1992–97

Shrink-wrapped in Type VI packaging; includes two insulating pins and instructions. **Cross-reference:** PW OSS.

CP

12925   O GAUGE O42 CURVED TRACK SECTION, 1996–97

Lionel created this track section in response to operators who wanted more radius than standard O gauge curved track (31"), yet needed a more compact oval because of layout area restrictions. Together with the O54 and O72 curved sections, the 12925 gives Lionel operators great flexibility in layout planning.

CP

O GAUGE SWITCHES, 1970–97

5132   REMOTE SWITCH, 1980–94

Right-hand switch, with lighted controller, interior illumination, and constant-voltage plug, essentially

Exc   Mint

identical to postwar units. Early runs of this switch were plagued with operating problems, but within a year the unit became quite reliable. Superseded by 23010-11 units in 1995. **Cross-reference:** PW 022.

40   45

5133   REMOTE SWITCH, 1980–94

Left-hand switch, with lighted controller, interior illumination, and constant-voltage plug, essentially identical to postwar units. Superseded by 23010-11 units in 1995. **Cross-reference:** PW 022.

40   45

5165   O72 WIDE-RADIUS REMOTE SWITCH, 1987–97

Left-hand switch with controller. This and its right-hand companion are revivals of the prewar 711 wide-radius switches; they should meet with great popularity.

CP

5166   O72 WIDE-RADIUS REMOTE SWITCH, 1987–97

Right-hand switch with controller.

CP

5193   THREE PAIR REMOTE SWITCHES, 1983

Three each of 5132 and 5133 switches with controllers.

240   270

23010   LEFT-HAND O31 SWITCH, 1994–97

Black all-plastic construction with rotating lens mechanism and black three-wire lighted controler. This switch and its companion (23011) represent new designs and replace the large 022 switches Lionel has always used for its O gauge track. Like its predecessors, the 23101 can operate from fixed or track voltage, features illumination (as does its controller), and has a nonderailing feature and a reversible lantern housing. In addition, the housing can be removed completely, though once taken out it cannot be reinstalled. This switch is also equipped for TrainMaster Command, which was probably the main reason for the redesign. It comes with two track extensions for a narrow or wide turnout application, so it possesses considerable flexibility. Reports from some operators have indicated that early versions had quality control problems with the movable frog rail, and a few have complained about the apparent fragility of the switch's construction. The 022

Exc   Mint

switches are still plentiful, so operators who prefer the older design have an alternative. With the extensions installed, this switch nicely matches the older versions. **Cross-references:** PW 022; ME 5132.

CP

23011 RIGHT-HAND O31 SWITCH, 1994–97

Black all-plastic construction with rotating lens mechanism and black three-wire illuminated controller. This switch and its companion (23010) represent new designs and replace the large 022 switches Lionel has always used for its O gauge track. Like its predecessors, the 23011 can operate from fixed or track voltage, features illumination (as does its controller), and has a nonderailing feature and a reversible lantern housing. In addition, the housing can be removed completely, although once taken out it cannot be reinstalled. This switch is also equipped for TrainMaster Command, which was probably the main reason for the redesign. It comes with two track extensions for a narrow or wide turnout application, so it possesses considerable flexibility. Reports from some operators have indicated that early versions had quality control. problems with the movable frog rail, and a few people have complained about the apparent fragility of the switch's construction. The 022 switches are still plentiful, so operators who prefer the older design have an alternative. With the extensions installed, this switch nicely matches the older versions. **Cross-references:** PW 022; ME 5133.

CP

TRUTRACK SYSTEM COMPONENTS, 1973–74

In 1973 and 1974, Fundimensions attempted a major innovation in its operating system with the introduction of Trutrack. This new system featured a realistic T-shaped rail made from aluminum, wood-grained plastic ties at relatively close intervals, wide-radius curves, and a thin, less conspicuous center rail. The track used a snap-lock assembly with rail joiners. Trutrack featured separate pieces of rubberized ballasted roadbed that snapped onto each track or switch piece. The ballasted roadbed is more plastic than rubber, but it is flexible.

The 1973 catalog listed remote and manual switches, switch roadbed, and lockons, as well as the straight and curved track sections and their roadbed pieces. In 1973 the right manual switches caused derailments because they would not lock tightly, so in 1974 the mechanism was changed and improved for the manual switches. Unfortunately, aluminum track is not compatible with Magnetraction. Although some sources have stated that Fundimensions had problems with the switches, which were supposed to have been made in

Exc   Mint

Italy, we suspect that the incompatibility with Magnetraction is the reason the track was dropped from production after only small amounts were produced, since Magnetraction was more important to Lionel's operating system than an improved track appearance.

We have updated our lists of Trutrack that actually reached production since our first edition; more was actually produced than was first believed. Values for this track are difficult to estimate, since it never reached production. These track pieces and switches are therefore listed as NRS until firm sales figures reach us.

5600 CURVED TRACK, 1973

Single piece of track.   **NRS**

5601 CARD OF FOUR CURVED TRACK, 1973

Pieces of track came fastened together with rubber band inside packaging.   **NRS**

5602 CARD OF FOUR ROADBED BALLAST, 1973–74

Pieces of roadbed for curved track came fastened together with rubber band inside packaging.   **NRS**

5605 STRAIGHT TRACK, 1973

Single piece of track.   **NRS**

5606 CARD OF FOUR STRAIGHT TRACK, 1973

Pieces of track came fastened together with rubber band inside packaging.   **NRS**

5607 CARD OF FOUR ROADBED BALLAST, 1973

Pieces of roadbed for straight track came fastened together with rubber band inside packaging, Type II packaging.   **NRS**

5620 MANUAL SWITCH, 1973–74

Left-hand switch not distributed for sale, but some became available. After first production run in 1973, mechanism was redesigned for second run in 1974.   **NRS**

5625 REMOTE SWITCH, 1973

Left-hand switch not distributed for sale, but some became available.   **NRS**

Engineers at Fundimensions developed the Trutrack System in 1973. Although samples exist, the components were never mass-produced.

	Exc	Mint

5630 MANUAL SWITCH, 1973–74

Right-hand switch not distributed for sale, but some became available. After first production run in 1973, mechanism was redesigned for second run in 1974.

NRS

5635 REMOTE SWITCH, 1973

Right-hand switch not distributed for sale, but some became available.

NRS

5640 CARD OF TWO SWITCH ROADBED PIECES, 1973

Pair of roadbed pieces to accommodate left-hand switches.

NRS

	Exc	Mint

5650 CARD OF TWO SWITCH ROADBED PIECES, 1973

Pair of roadbed pieces to accommodate right-hand switches.

NRS

5655 LOCKON, 1973

Device connects to track to bring power from transformer.

NRS

5660 CARD OF TERMINAL TRACK WITH LOCKON, 1973

Special track equipped with device to bring power from transformer.

NRS

12
PERIPHERALS

The shack was in the angel's seat of the ape wagon, blowing smoke to the Big-O of the time he was a baby-lifter on the varnish. Or, to say it another way: The brakeman was in the cupola of the caboose, boasting to the conductor of the time he was a brakeman on a passenger train.
— B. A. Botkin and Alvin F. Harlow, Eds.,
A Treasury of Railroad Folklore

INTRODUCTION

Peripherals, as their name suggests, are not really part of the mainstream of Lionel production. However, they constitute a fascinating part of the Lionel story. The first true peripherals were probably the ready-made layouts Lionel sold to dealers for storefront window displays; after all, that's how Joshua Lionel Cowen first conceived of his little creations when he founded the company. Other items were the many premiums made for Lionel employees and the commemorative pieces made for the firm's golden anniversary celebration in 1950.

In the modern era, the story of peripheral items begins with the 75th anniversary items produced for sale, although some of the Johnny Cash items made in 1972 could qualify as well. In 1975, Fundimensions produced an astonishing variety of Lionel commemoratives: window stickers, playing cards, belt buckles, posters, clocks, and even an authentic Lionel-embossed kerosene lantern, a highly prized item today. After that celebration, not much attention was given to the peripheral market until Richard Kughn took over the firm in 1986 as Lionel Trains Inc. Kughn and his advisers saw that many aftermarket manufacturers were marketing keepsakes that used Lionel's logos and symbols. Since this practice infringed on copyright, Lionel's new directors put these manufacturers on notice that any unauthorized marketing of products with Lionel trademarks would be vigorously prosecuted. Most dealers complied by securing Lionel's permission, for a price. Others were in fact prosecuted.

In 1987 the reason for this sudden enforcement in an area neglected by Fundimensions became clear. In a separate catalog, LTI announced its new SideTracks lines of keepsakes and souvenirs to be marketed by Lionel itself. These items, from T-shirts and ties to pen and pencil sets, were subcontracted and marketed through Lionel's existing dealer network or by special order. Since 1987, a wide variety of items has been marketed, not all of which have been cataloged. Because the marketing strategy for these peripherals has been different from the marketing of the trains themselves, we expect that the listings presented here are incomplete. To further confuse the matter, many of these peripherals bear no catalog number, especially the eagerly sought 1975 anniversary items. For the items produced from 1987 through the present, we have supplied a simple listing, since it has been difficult to determine the going prices for these items, aside from Lionel's original asking price. For example, it is known that none of the Christmas ornaments, lighted or nonilluminated, sells for more than $5, and many of them have been sold for as little as three for $10. In the next few years, it is possible that a collector market will be established for the SideTracks items.

The following listings are divided into three parts: Items produced before 1987, items produced after 1987, and SideTracks items from 1987 onward. Reader input is requested as to values of the newer items and completeness of these lists.

PERIPHERALS PRODUCED BEFORE 1987

1355 TRAIN DISPLAY CASE, 1983

— 40

2951 TRACK LAYOUT BOOK, 1976–80 and 1983

Several editions have been issued; see listings in *Greenberg's Guide to Lionel Paper and Collectibles* for full information.

2   5

2952 TRACK ACCESSORY MANUAL, 1976–80 and 1983

Several editions have been issued; see listings in *Greenberg's Guide to Lionel Paper and Collectibles* for full information.

2   5

2953 TRAIN AND ACCESSORY MANUAL, 1977–85

Several editions have been issued; see listings in *Greenberg's Guide to Lionel Paper and Collectibles* for full information.

2   5

2960 LIONEL 75TH ANNIVERSARY BOOK, 1975

Blue cover with 75th anniversary logo, came in white wrapper-box with black-printed white label; mint value includes box. In retrospect, this is an interesting document despite many inaccuracies known to collectors even at the time of its publication.

10   15

2985 LIONEL TRAIN BOOK, 1986–97

Lionel's most ambitious effort to date to provide a recent "starter" book for operators. Several editions have been issued; see listings in *Greenberg's Guide to Lionel Paper and Collectibles* for full information.

CP

JC-1 LIONEL JOHNNY CASH RECORD ALBUM, 1972–75

33⅓ RPM album, one of many Johnny Cash items marketed by Lionel. As a further note, the 1974 television production, *Johnny Cash: Ridin' the Rails*, sponsored by Lionel, is available on videotape (Sony B0241VH).

10   12

7-1100 HAPPY HUFF 'N PUFF, 1975

Push toy train for preschool-age children similar to sets made by Fisher-Price and Playskool; whimsical old-fashioned four-wheel steamer and two gondolas embossed with two large squares on their sides. Train is made of plastic simulated to look like wood. Wheels fastened with metal axles. Locomotive has smiling mouth and eye decorations. Came with a circle of two-rail plastic track and a story booklet showing how

Happy Huff 'N Puff got his name. Also includes special Huff 'N Puff booklet.

40   60

7-1200 GRAVEL GUS, 1975

Three-piece road construction set consisting of a grader with large, square head seated on the chassis (presumably Gus) and two side dump cars. The grader has four large wheels and swivels in the center with a removable pusher blade. Each car has one axle with two large wheels; the first car rests on the grader, the second car rests on the rear of the first. The set, which was made from plastic simulated to resemble wood, came with a full-color story booklet.

20   40

7-1300 GRAVEL GUS JUNIOR, 1975

Appears to be identical to 7-1200, but with only one car.

15   30

7-1400 HAPPY HUFF 'N PUFF JUNIOR, 1975

Similar to 7-1100, except does not include circle of track, locomotive has much thicker smokestack, and gondolas are not embossed with large squares. These four preschool-age toys apparently were offered only in 1975 through large toy outlets. Their success would have been an asset to Fundimensions, but they were launched into the teeth of a highly competitive market long dominated by giants such as Fisher-Price and Playskool. By the 1990s, the market had changed considerably, and Lionel successfully jumped in with its large scale Thomas the Tank Engine set, which became the biggest-selling train set in Lionel's history.

40   65

2390 LIONEL MIRROR, 1982

Old-fashioned mirror with dark walnut wood frame, gold, red, and black decoration showing 1920s-era picture of Lawrence Cowen with train set at base of antiqued gold archway. Gold lettering, "LIONEL ELECTRIC TRAINS, THE STANDARD OF THE WORLD SINCE 1900". Also "COPYRIGHT 1981 GPC".

65   90

[NO NUMBER] BELT BUCKLE, 1981

Solid antique brass, Lionel logo. Over the years, several versions of this belt buckle have been made,

Exc   Mint

some round and others oval. Reader input is requested concerning specific varieties and years of production.

15   20

[NO NUMBER] LIONEL CLOCK, 1976–77

White dial with black hour and minute hands, red second hand, red field on bottom with white "LIONEL"; made by American Sign & Advertising Services Inc., 7430 Industrial Rd., Industrial Park, Lawrence KY, 41042, and available to Service Stations for $20 to $25. A clock made the year before is similar to this version, but it is neon-lighted and has the 75th anniversary logo (black locomotive front). Other dealer clocks and neon signs have been made; reader input as to specific types is requested.

100   175

[NO NUMBER] LIONEL PENNANT

Measures 45" wide and 29½" high; plastic, white background, black trim on edge, black "LIONEL" and "A LIFETIME INVESTMENT IN HAPPINESS", left arrow is red, right arrow blue. This design is a possible carryover from late postwar era.

25   35

[NO NUMBER] BLACK CAVE VINYL PLAYMAT, 1982

Measures 30" x 40", included in 1254 Black Cave Flyer set.

5   10

[NO NUMBER] COMMANDO ASSAULT TRAIN PLAYMAT, 1983

Measures 30" x 40"; included in 1355 Commando Assault Train set.

5   10

[NO NUMBER] ROCKY MOUNTAIN FREIGHT PLAYMAT, 1983

Measures 36" x 54"; included in 1352 Rocky Mountain Freight set.

5   10

[NO NUMBER] CANNONBALL FREIGHT VINYL PLAYMAT, 1982

Two-piece mat measuring 36" x 54"; included in 1155 Cannonball Freight set.

5   10

[NO NUMBER] L. A. S. E. R. VINYL PLAYMAT, 1981–82

Measures 36" x 54"; included in 1150 L. A. S. E. R. Train set.

5   10

[NO NUMBER] LIONEL PLAYING CARDS, 1975

Regulation 52-card poker deck, red and black diagonal Lionel logo, head-on locomotive front against background in black, wrapped in cellophane and packaged in silver and black box.

3   5

[NO NUMBER] STATION PLATFORM, 1983

Measures 23" x 3½" x 5"; included in 1351 Baltimore & Ohio set; similar to 2256 Station Platform. Details requested.

7   10

[NO NUMBER] WRIST WATCH, 1986

Gold-plated case, gold dial face with circle of "track" around which a small General-type steam train revolves as it functions as the second hand; red, white, and blue Lionel logo on dial face, alligator-style leather wrist band. Special offer to members of Lionel Railroader Club; they could obtain one for $99.95, including shipping and handling.

—   120

[NO NUMBER] RAILROAD LANTERN, 1975

Regulation kerosene-burning railroad lantern with clear lens, bright galvanized unfinished surfaces, stamped "LIONEL" atop upper lid. This hard-to-find peripheral is the most prized of all the 75th anniversary items.

175   225

PERIPHERALS PRODUCED AFTER 1987

12752 HISTORICAL LIONEL VIDEOTAPE, 1989–91

VHS format videotape of Lionel history; 1989 package features portrait of Joshua Lionel Cowen in catalog, but production videos have brown cover with Santa Fe F3 diesel and white lettering.

20   25

12756 **A LIONEL TOUR: THE MAKING OF THE SCALE HUDSON, 1991**

VHS format videotape showing the manufacturing process for the new version of the full-scale New York Central Hudson. Cover sleeve has photo of Hudson, red lettering, and Lionel logo.

20   25

12821 **LIONEL CATALOG VIDEO, 1992**

VHS format videotape showing 1992 Lionel catalog items in operation.

20   25

12887 **LIONEL DISPLAY CONDUCTOR FIGURE, 1995**

This imposing dealer display was to be a virtual duplicate of one made during the late prewar years; it would have been nearly life-size and featured an illuminated swinging lantern. Apparently preliminary market surveys discouraged its production because of its expense.

Not Manufactured

16901 **LIONEL CATALOG VIDEO, 1991**

VHS format videotape showing 1991 Lionel catalog items in operation.

20   25

23002-09 AND **23012** **OPERATING ROLLER BASE DISPLAYS, 1993–94**

These are display bases with rollers and connections for a transformer so that a locomotive can be run while stationary. Powered bases of this nature were also made in the mid-1930s to demonstrate the then-new Lionel whistles in tenders. The differing numbers refer to sizes for small to very large locomotives.

—   120

33001 **RAILSCOPE DEALER PROMOTIONAL SET, 1991**

This dealer display came knocked down in a cardboard outer wrapper and a packing box. It consisted of the RailScope television, a cardboard placard, a large scale figure of an engineer, literature and instruction sheets, and a special promotional video.

—   150

33002 **RAILSCOPE BLACK-AND-WHITE TELEVISION, 1991**

Small black-and-white television with display stand, power pack, and antenna; red case with Lionel logo. Meant to display RailScope images, also worked as ordinary TV; priced about $25 more than its non-Lionel equivalent at time of release.

50   75

SIDE-TRACKS ITEMS PRODUCED BETWEEN 1987 AND 1995

Many other Lionel items have been produced either through license or directly by Lionel. Among these are a golf umbrella, leather jacket, playing cards, bowling towel, and even boxer shorts. The items listed here refer only to those that have been cataloged by Lionel and assigned a catalog number.

5800 **BUMPER STICKER**

Measures 3" x 14", Lionel logo, black Made In America on white background with black locomotive pilot.

—   1.50

5801 **LIGHTER, 1987–90**

Disposable white butane lighter with Lionel logo and black Lionel Lines lettering.

—   3.50

5802 **LAPEL PIN, 1987–91**

Enameled red, white, and blue Lionel logo.

—   4

5803 **LICENSE PLATE, 1987 and 1991**

White background, dark blue edges, red and blue lettering and Lionel logo, red and black freight train.

—   4

5804 **EPOXY KEY CHAIN, 1987**

Red, white, and blue Lionel logo screened and epoxied onto brass 24k gold-plated medallion attached to brass key ring.

—   4.50

5805 ASH TRAY, 1987–90

Triangular 3½" glass ash tray with red, white, and blue Lionel logo.

—   6.50

5806 COFFEE MUG, 1987–90

12-ounce black ironstone mug with gold rim and gold Lionel logo.

—   7.50

5807 SPORT CAP, 1987

Red cap with Lionel logo inside white rectangle.

—   8

5808 BRASS KEY CHAIN, 1987–90

Lionel logo and steam engine boiler front stamped into brass-finished medallion.

—   8

5809 ENGINEER'S GLOVES, 1987

Work gloves with gray cowhide palms, thumb, fingers, and knuckle straps; blue denim collars and backs; black Lionel logo and lettering on glove collars.

—   8.50

5810 SLEEPING BOY POSTER, 1987

R. Tyrrell poster from 1980 catalog; poster measures 21" x 27".

—   9

5811 NICKEL PLATE SPECIAL POSTER, 1987

Black border, painting of Nickel Plate Road freight, "BIG, RUGGED TRAINS SINCE 1900" lettering, measures 20" x 34".

—   9

5812 RAIL BLAZER POSTER, 1987

Red border, painting of Rail Blazer tank locomotive and freight train, "No Childhood Should Be Without A Train" lettering, measures 20" x 34".

—   9

5813 T-SHIRT, 1987

Small blue shirt with rectangular red, white, and blue Lionel logo.

—   11

5814 T-SHIRT, 1987

Medium blue shirt with rectangular red, white, and blue Lionel logo.

—   11

5815 T-SHIRT, 1987

Large blue shirt with rectangular red, white, and blue Lionel logo.

—   11

5816 T-SHIRT, 1987

Extra-large blue shirt with rectangular red, white, and blue Lionel logo.

—   11

5817 PORTABLE TOOL KIT, 1987

Thirteen-in-one ratchet-socket screwdriver folding set, black storage handle, red, blue, and chrome Lionel logo, chromed attachment piece.

—   11.50

5818 MINI-MAG-LITE FLASHLIGHT, 1987

5½" long, with engraved Lionel logo and steam engine boiler front on black metal flashlight body.

—   20

5819 PEN AND PENCIL SET, 1987–90

Black matte barrels, chrome-trimmed, red, white, and blue Lionel logo on cap ends, silver "LIONEL TRAINS" embossed into barrels.

—   20

5820 TRAVEL ALARM CLOCK, 1987

Red plastic case, quartz movement, dial with circle of track and General train moving around track, red, white, and blue Lionel logo.

—   20

5821 BEVERAGE COASTER SET, 1987

Polished solid brass coasters with brown leather insert and central Lionel medallion, felt bottoms, oak holding tray.

— 70

5822 WRIST WATCH, 1987

Gold-plated case and band, black watch hands, dial has circle of track with Southern Pacific *Daylight* steam engine and car moving around track to function as second hand; red, white, and blue Lionel logo on dial face.

— 110

5823 "LIONEL/THE LEGEND LIVES ON!", 1989–90

Bumper sticker with white background, gray photo of prewar train, red and blue lettering with Lionel logo.

— 1.50

5824 LIONEL NOTEPADS, 1989–90

Two pads measuring 3" x 5" with 100 sheets each, white paper with light lavender circle-L logo and words "Official Lionel Enthusiast".

— 2.50

5825 LIONEL FABRIC PATCH, 1989–91

Measures 3" in diameter, red, white and blue circle-L logo with black outlines.

— 3

5826 LIONEL PENNANT, 1989–91

Triangular pennant, red with white outline "LIONEL" and circle-L logo.

— 4.50

5827 AMERICAN FLYER PENNANT, 1989–91

Triangular pennant, blue with white American Flyer in script.

— 4.50

5828 "I BRAKE FOR LIONEL TRAINS!" LICENSE PLATE, 1989–91

Black background, white and red lettering, circle-L logo, white and red striped crossing gate and signal.

— 4.50

5829 LIONEL LAPEL PIN, 1989–91

Brass pin with red and blue Lionel lettering and circle-L logo.

— 4.50

5830 AMERICAN FLYER LAPEL PIN, 1989–91

Brass pin with blue American Flyer lettering on silver background.

— 4.50

5831 BEVERAGE CAN HOLDERS, 1989–90

Set of one red and one blue polyurethane holders, each having white Lionel lettering and white outline circle-L logo.

— 5.50

5832 LIONEL CARPENTER'S APRON, 1989–90

White canvas apron with red Lionel lettering and circle-L logo.

— 7

5833 AMERICAN FLYER CARPENTER'S APRON, 1989–90

White canvas apron with blue American Flyer script.

— 7

5834 BEVERAGE MUG, 1989–91

Thirteen-ounce glass mug with diesel and steam locomotives on either side of red Lionel lettering and circle-L logo.

(A) 1989–90: frosted glass mug.

— 8.50

(B) 1991: clear glass mug.

— 8.50

5835 ENGINEER'S CAP, 1989–91

Gray and white striped cap with red, white, and blue circle-L logo patch.

— 9

5836 T-SHIRT, 1989–90

Small blue child's shirt with red, white, and blue circle-L logo.

—   11

5837 T-SHIRT, 1989–90

Medium blue child's shirt with red, white, and blue circle-L logo.

—   11

5838 T-SHIRT, 1989–90

Large blue child's shirt with red, white, and blue circle-L logo.

—   11

5839 T-SHIRT, 1989–90

Small white adult's shirt with red, white, and blue circle-L logo.

—   11

5840 T-SHIRT, 1989–90

Medium white adult's shirt with red, white, and blue circle-L logo.

—   11

5841 T-SHIRT, 1989–90

Large white adult's shirt with red, white, and blue circle-L logo.

—   11

5842 T-SHIRT, 1989–90

Extra-large white adult's shirt with red, white, and blue circle-L logo.

—   11

5843 POSTERS, 1989–90

Set of three large posters: "Sleeping Boy" from R. J. Tyrrell drawing of 1980, "Nickel Plate Special" and "Rail Blazer."

—   15

5844 SWEATSHIRT, 1989–90

Small red child's sweatshirt with Lionel lettering and logo.

—   16

5845 SWEATSHIRT, 1989–90

Medium red child's sweatshirt with Lionel lettering and logo.

—   16

5846 SWEATSHIRT, 1989–90

Large red child's sweatshirt with Lionel lettering and logo.

—   16

5847 LIONEL TOTE BAG, 1989–91

Bright red nylon bag with white outline Lionel lettering and circle-L logo.

—   15.50

5848 AMERICAN FLYER TOTE BAG, 1989–91

Bright blue nylon bag with white American Flyer script.

—   15.50

5849 SWEATSHIRT, 1989–90

Small red adult's sweatshirt with Lionel lettering and logo.

—   16

5850 SWEATSHIRT, 1989–90

Medium red adult's sweatshirt with Lionel lettering and logo.

—   16

5851 SWEATSHIRT, 1989–90

Large red adult's sweatshirt with Lionel lettering and logo.

—   16

5852 SWEATSHIRT, 1989–90

Extra-large red adult's sweatshirt with Lionel lettering and logo.

—   16

5853 MAN'S TIE, 1989–90

Dark blue man's tie with small white circle-L logos.

—   22

5854 WOMAN'S TIE, 1989–90

Dark blue woman's bow tie with white circle-L logos.

— 22

5855 POCKET KNIFE, 1989–91

Black plastic handle, two knife blades, tweezers, toothpick, and key ring; Lionel lettering and circle-L logo inlaid in nickel.

— 25

5856 POCKET WATCH, 1989–90

Nickel-plated case, engraving of General locomotive on back, white face with red Lionel logo and black numerals.

— 26

5857 WELCOME MAT, 1989–90

Blue mat on black pad with red and white Lionel lettering and circle-L logo.

— 30

5858 DIRECTOR'S CHAIR, 1989–91

Varnished pine frame, white canvas seat and back, red Lionel lettering, and red and blue circle-L logo on back.

— 60

5859 LIONEL ELECTRIC TRAINS PENNANT, 1991

Triangular pennant, orange with classic rectangular cream, orange, and blue "LIONEL ELECTRIC TRAINS" logo.

— 4.50

5860 ALL ABOARD COOKBOOK, 1991

350 family recipes from Lionel Corporation employees; white front cover with red checkerboard border, blue lettering, gray place setting where dish is formed from red, white, and blue circle-L logo.

NRS

5861 T-SHIRT, 1991

Small white child's shirt with steam engine coming out of tunnel on front and SP-type caboose going into tunnel on back; back and front have red Lionel Trains lettering and circle-L logo.

— 11

5862 T-SHIRT, 1991

Medium white child's shirt with steam engine coming out of tunnel on front and SP-type caboose going into tunnel on back; back and front have red Lionel Trains lettering and circle-L logo.

— 11

5863 T-SHIRT, 1991

Large white child's shirt with steam engine coming out of tunnel on front and SP-type caboose going into tunnel on back; back and front have red Lionel Trains lettering and circle-L logo.

— 11

5864 T-SHIRT, 1991

Small white adult's shirt with steam engine coming out of tunnel on front and SP-type caboose going into tunnel on back; back and front have red Lionel Trains lettering and circle-L logo.

— 11

5865 T-SHIRT, 1991

Medium white adult's shirt with steam engine coming out of tunnel on front and SP-type caboose going into tunnel on back; back and front have red Lionel Trains lettering and circle-L logo.

— 11

5866 T-SHIRT, 1991

Large white adult's shirt with steam engine coming out of tunnel on front and SP-type caboose going into tunnel on back; back and front have red Lionel Trains lettering and circle-L logo.

— 11

5867 T-SHIRT, 1991

Extra-large white adult's shirt with steam engine coming out of tunnel on front and SP-type caboose going into tunnel on back; back and front have red Lionel Trains lettering and circle-L logo.

— 11

Exc   Mint

5868 BUMPER STICKER, 1991

Black outline steam locomotive, red Lionel lettering and circle-L logo, American flag at right.
—   1.50

5869 CHRISTMAS ORNAMENT, 1991

Porcelain multicolored painted tank locomotive with white Lionel lettering and circle-L logo.
—   4

5870 CHRISTMAS ORNAMENT, 1991

Porcelain multicolored wood-sided caboose with white Lionel lettering and circle-L logo.
—   4

5871 CHRISTMAS ORNAMENT, 1991

Porcelain multicolored freight and passenger station with white Lionel lettering and circle-L logo.
—   4

5872 CHRISTMAS ORNAMENT, 1991

Porcelain multicolored figure of boy-engineer holding lantern.
—   4

5873 OLD WORLD CHRISTMAS ORNAMENT, 1991

Porcelain multicolored figure of Santa Claus holding toy locomotive.
—   4

5874 CHRISTMAS ORNAMENT, 1991

Porcelain multicolored crossing warning signal with white Lionel lettering.
—   4

5875 STUFFED ANIMAL, 1991

Lenny the Lionel Lion, 11"-high doll dressed in blue and white-striped engineer's cap and overalls, white gloves, and red and white bandanna.
—   20

Exc   Mint

5876 MAN'S TIE, 1991

Maroon man's tie with small white circle-L logos.
—   22

5877 WOMAN'S TIE, 1991

Maroon woman's bow tie with white circle-L logos.
—   22

5878 SPORT CAP, 1991

Dark blue cap and visor with white front, red Lionel lettering and circle-L logo.
—   16

5879 "10 DECADES OF TRAINING" BUMPER STICKER, 1992

Orange bumper sticker with rectangular Lionel logo and block script in blue.
—   2

5880 AMERICAN FLYER FABRIC PATCH, 1992

Badge-shaped sew-on patch with red, white, and blue American Flyer block lettering.
—   3

5882 LIONEL/AMERICAN FLAG LAPEL PIN, 1992

Brass pin with Lionel and American flag crossed flags.
—   4

5892 CHRISTMAS ORNAMENT, 1992

Limited-production, numbered Christmas ornament featuring Lionel logo, number of run, and picture of 700E Hudson with two kittens.
—   5

5893 NEWSPAPER CARRIER BAG, 1992

Large orange canvas bag, 19" x 12½" x 8", with blue, orange, and white rectangular "Lionel Electric Trains" logo.
NRS

5897 MAN'S WATCH, 1992

Quartz watch; dial has red, white, and blue Lionel circle-L logo, gold-colored case, black leather band.
— 30

5898 WOMAN'S WATCH, 1992

Quartz watch; dial has red, white, and blue circle-L Lionel logo, gold-colored case, black leather band.
— 30

5899 CHRISTMAS ORNAMENT SET, 1992

Multicolored locomotive, passenger coach, and caboose ornaments lit through hole in base; socket takes any small Christmas tree lamp from standard set.
— 10

5900 CHRISTMAS ORNAMENT SET, 1992

Multicolored Santa Claus, little boy, and crossing signal nonilluminated ornaments.
— 10

5901 CHRISTMAS ORNAMENT SET, 1992

Multicolored 381E locomotive, station, and circus caboose ornaments lit through hole in base.
— 10

5902 CHRISTMAS ORNAMENT SET, 1992

Multicolored flatcar with elves and gifts, Lenny the Lion figure, and visored baseball cap nonilluminated ornaments.
— 10

5903 CHRISTMAS ORNAMENT SET, 1992

Small old-time steam locomotive, Santa Fe F3 diesel, and 700E Hudson pewter ornaments.
NRS

5904 CHRISTMAS ORNAMENT SET, 1993

One blue and one yellow locomotive nonilluminated ornaments.
— 7

5905 CHRISTMAS ORNAMENT SET, 1993

Three thin metal gold-finished ornaments: round with Lionel boy encircled by track, old-time steam locomotive, and Tyrrell "little boy sleeping" theme.
NRS

5906 PHOTOGRAPH FRAME, 1993

Rectangular 5" x 7" walnut photograph frame with engraved locomotive figures around its perimeter.
NRS

5907 WOVEN THROW RUG, 1993

Light gray 60" x 42" cotton throw rug decorated with black Berkshire steam locomotive and Lionel circle-L and block script logos. **NRS**

5908 THE MIGHTY SANTA FE BOOK, 1993

Hardbound, 32-page children's book written by William H. Hooks and illustrated by Angela Trotta Thomas; cover features boy looking over Lionel layout.
— 16

5909 CHRISTMAS ORNAMENT SET, 1993

Multicolored steam locomotive, passenger coach, and caboose nonilluminated ornaments.
— 10

5913 CHRISTMAS ORNAMENT SET, 1993

Multicolored 381E electric locomotive, station house, and circus caboose nonilluminated ornaments.
— 10

5914 RUGBY SHIRT, 1993

Small long-sleeve collared rugby shirt available in black, blue, or gray with embroidered Lionel script and circle-L logo.
— 25

5915 RUGBY SHIRT, 1993

Medium long-sleeve collared rugby shirt available in black, blue, or gray with embroidered Lionel script and circle-L logo.
— 25

5916 RUGBY SHIRT, 1993

Large long-sleeve collared rugby shirt available in black, blue, or gray with embroidered Lionel script and circle-L logo.

— 25

5917 RUGBY SHIRT, 1993

Extra-large long-sleeve collared rugby shirt available in black, blue, or gray with embroidered Lionel script and circle-L logo.

— 25

5918 RUGBY SHIRT, 1993

Extra-extra-large long-sleeve collared rugby shirt available in black, blue, or gray with embroidered Lionel script and circle-L logo.

— 25

About the Author

Roland E. LaVoie, 53, a native of the Philadelphia area, has been an avid toy train collector and writer for the last twenty years. He is a graduate of two of the area's schools: Bishop Eustace Preparatory School in Pennsauken, New Jersey, and LaSalle University in Philadelphia. As a youth in his home town of Collingswood, New Jersey, he vividly remembers seeing the last of the great K4s steam-driven passenger trains on the old Pennsylvania-Reading Seashore Lines tracks.

In real life, LaVoie has been a teacher of English for the last thirty years, most of them at Cherry Hill High School East in Cherry Hill, New Jersey. As such, he has written poetry, collected books, and acquired an extensive library of classic motion pictures on videotape. He has been a feature of the local Greenberg train shows, where he exercises his teaching skills by conducting demonstrations and clinics with his crowded 5 x 8-foot Lionel layout. LaVoie also has edited a number of Greenberg price guides and written *Model Railroading with Lionel Trains*. He lives in a large, rambling home in Cherry Hill with his wife, Jimmie; son, Tom; mother-in-law, Louise; and an astonishing variety of rescue dogs—two beagles and two Labrador mixes—and a very apprehensive cat!

INDEX

Numbers in *italics* indicate a photograph or illustration on the page indicated.

12866	133, *134*	12894	61	12929	37	23002-09	149
12867	*134*	12895	61	12931	100	23010	143
12868	*134*	12896	70	12932	110	23011	144
12869	109, *111*	12897	98	12935	110	23012	149
12873	33	12898	83	12936	37	33001	149
12874	46	12899	46	12937	37	33002	149
12875	109, *110*	12900	99	12938	136	52021	*110,* 112
12877	34	12901	99	12939	136	52025	*112*
12878	25	12902	35, *36*	12948	70	52028	112
12880	*135*	12903	83	12951	100	52033	112
12881	110	12904	99	12952	100	52039	126
12882	46	12905	99	12953	100	52053	*113*
12883	61	12906	100	12954	100	52055	*112,* 113
12884	98	12907	110	12958	37	52056	113
12885	135, *126*	12911	136	12960	26	52069	*113*
12886	46	12912	35	12962	83	52091	113
12887	149	12914	136	15906	126	52100	26
12888	*51,* 56	12915	36	16357	111	7-1100	147
12889	*82*	12916	36	16383	111	7-1200	147
12890	*134,* 135	12917	25	16398	111	7-1300	147
12891	110, *111*	12921	26	16901	149	7-1400	147
12892	56	12925	143	17894	111	JC-1	147
12893	136	12927	46	17896	111	UCS	142